THE EIGHTH CRUSADE

By

ALEXANDRE DUMAS

Originally published by Hurst and Company, New York 1900.
Typeset and republished by Cavalier Books, Milwaukee 2014.
Cover: The Battle of the Pyramids by François-Louis-Joseph Watteau, 1799.

ISBN: 0991560647
ISBN-13: 978-0-9915606-4-6

CAVALIER BOOKS

This edition copyright © 2014 by Cavalier Books, Milwaukee, Wisconsin. All rights reserved. With the exception of short excerpts for critical reviews, no part of this book may be reproduced or transmitted in any form or by any means whatsoever without permission in writing from the publisher.

CONTENTS

CHAPTER I 1
CHAPTER II 8
CHAPTER III 15
CHAPTER IV 21
CHAPTER V 27
CHAPTER VI 35
CHAPTER VII 42
CHAPTER VIII 48
CHAPTER IX 55
CHAPTER X 61
CHAPTER XI 69
CHAPTER XII 74
CHAPTER XIII 79
CHAPTER XIV 84
CHAPTER XV 89
CHAPTER XVI 96
CHAPTER XVII 103
CHAPTER XVIII 109
CHAPTER XIX 117

CHAPTER I

SAINT JEAN D'ACRE

On the 7th of April, 1799, the promontory on which Saint Jean d'Acre—the Ptolemais of ancient times—stands, was enveloped in as much thunder and lightning as Mount Sinai on the day the Lord issued the law to Moses from the burning bush.

Whence came these deafening reverberations that shook the coast of Syria as if by an earthquake?

Whence came this smoke that covered the Gulf of Carmel with a cloud as thick as if Mount Elias had been suddenly transformed into a volcano?

The dream of one of those men who change the destiny of nations with a word was accomplished.

We are wrong; we should have said, had vanished, or, rather, had changed to a reality, of which this man, ambitious as he was, had not dared to dream.

On the 10th of September, 1797, the conqueror of Italy, hearing at Passeriano of the 18th Fructidor, and the edict which condemned two members of the Directorate, fifty-four deputies, and one hundred and forty-eight private individuals to exile, relapsed into a profound reverie.

He was doubtless calculating in his own mind the influence this *coup d'etat*—which his own hand had directed, though Augereau had been apparently the sole factor—would have upon him personally.

He was walking with his secretary, Bourrienne, in the beautiful park connected with the palace, and suddenly raising his head, he said to him, without any preamble whatever:

"Europe is but a molehill. There has never been any great empire or revolution except in the East, where there are six hundred millions of men."

Then as Bourrienne, wholly unprepared for this outburst, gazed at him in astonishment, he again seemed to lose himself in thought.

On the 1st of January, 1798, Bonaparte, who had received an ovation at the theater on the first representation of "Horatio Cocles," and who had been greeted by shouts of "Long live Bonaparte!" that shook the building to its very foundations, returned to his house on the Rue de la Victoire—newly named in his honor the Rue de la Victoire—in a melancholy mood, remarking to Bourrienne, whom he often made the confidant of his gloomy thoughts:

"Take my word for it, Bourrienne, nobody in Paris remembers anything long. If I should not do anything for six months I should be ruined. One hero supersedes another in this modern Babylon, and I shall not attend the theater three times before the people cease to look for me."

Again, on the 29th of the same month, he said to Bourrienne, reverting incessantly to the ambitious dream that engrossed his mind:

"Bourrienne, I will not stay here. There is nothing for me to do. If I do stay I am undone, for everything in Europe seems to go to seed. This contracted little Europe does not furnish scope enough for me. I must go to the East."

Finally, on the 18th of April, 1798, about a fortnight before his departure, a he was walking down the Rue Saint Anne with Bourrienne, to whom he had not addressed a word since they left the Rue Chantereine, the secretary, to break the oppressive silence, said:

"And you have really decided to leave France, general?"

"Yes," replied Bonaparte. "I asked to be made one of them, and they refused. If I remain here I shall be obliged to overthrow them and make myself king. The nobles would not consent to that; I have sounded them. The time has not yet come; I should have no support. I must dazzle these people; so we will go to Egypt, Bourrienne."

So it was not to open communication with Tippo Sahib across Asia, or to wage war upon England in India, that Bonaparte left Europe.

The French people must be dazzled. That was the real object of Bonaparte's expedition to Egypt.

On the 3d of May, 1798, he ordered the embarkation of all the troops.

On the 4th he left Paris.

On the 8th he reached Toulon.

On the 19th he went aboard the "Orient," the admiral's vessel.

On the 25th he sighted Leghorn and the Island of Elba.

On the 13th of June he took Malta.

On the 19th he set sail again.

On the first of July he landed near Marabout.

On the 3d he carried Alexandria by assault.

On the 13th he won the battle of Chebreiss.

On the 21st he crushed the Mamelukes at the Pyramids.

On the 25th he entered Cairo.

On the 14th of August he received news of the defeat of Aboukir.

On the 24th he started, in company with several members of the Institute, to visit the remains of the Suez Canal.

On the 28th he drank at the fountain of Moses, and, like Pharaoh, narrowly escaped being drowned in the Red Sea.

On the 1st of January, 1799, he planned his Syrian campaign, though the idea had been conceived six months before, for at that time he had written to Kléber:

"If the English continue to overrun the Mediterranean,

they will perhaps compel us to do even greater things than we intended."

There had been vague rumors of an expedition which the Sultan of Damascus was fiting out against the French, and in which Djezzar Pasha—surnamed the Butcher, on account of his cruelty—had command of the advance guard.

These rumors had now assumed definite shape.

Djezzar had already advanced, by way of Gaza, as far as El-Arich, and had there massacred the few French officers in that fortress.

Among Bonaparte's young ordnance officers were the two Mailly brothers of Chateau Renaud. He dispatched the younger with a flag of truce to Djezzar, who, in defiance of all international law, made the messenger a prisoner.

This was a declaration of war, and Bonaparte, with his usual quickness of decision, resolved to destroy this advance guard of the Ottoman Porte.

In case he was successful in this attempt, he had other plans which he himself will divulge later on. If repulsed, he could still destroy the defense of Gaza, Jaffa, and Acre, lay waste the country, and destroy all the supplies, thus making it impossible for even a native army to cross the desert.

On the 11th of February, 1799, Bonaparte entered Syria at the head of twelve thousand men. He was attended by that galaxy of brave men that gravitated around him during the first and most brilliant period of his life.

He had Kléber, the handsomest and bravest horseman in the army.

He had Murat, who disputed this twofold title with Kléber.

He had Junot, who was such a wonderful shot with a pistol that he could split a dozen bullets in succession poised on the blade of a knife.

He had Lannes, who had earned his title of Duke of Montebello, but who had not yet assumed it.

He had Reynier, who was to have the honor of deciding the day at Heliopolis.

He had Caffarelli, who was destined to lie in the trench he had caused to be dug for his enemies.

And he also had as aid-de-camp our young Strasburg acquaintance, Eugene de Beauharnais, who had brought about the marriage between Josephine and Bonaparte by coming to ask the latter for his father's sword.

He had Croisier, who had been gloomy and taciturn ever since he had faltered in an encounter with the Arabs, and the word "Coward" had escaped Bonaparte's lips.

He had the elder of the two Maillys, who was resolved to either deliver or avenge his brother.

He had the young Sheik of Aher, Chief of the Druses, whose renown, if not his power, extended from the Dead Sea to the Mediterranean.

And last, but not least, he had an old acquaintance of ours, Roland de Montreval, whose natural intrepidity had, since the day he was wounded and taken prisoner at Cairo, been increased twofold by that strange desire for death we have seen him evince through the whole of our romance entitled "The Companions of Jehu."

On the 17th of February the army reached El-Arich.

The men had suffered greatly from thirst during the march. Only at Messoudiah—that is to say, the Favored Spot, had they found either refreshment or amusement. The soil at this point consisted of small dunes of exceedingly fine sand, and chance led a soldier to imitate the example of Moses and thrust a stick down into the sand. The water gushed out, as from an artesian well; the soldier tasted it, and found it excellent, so he called his comrades to share the fruits of his discovery with him. Each man then pinched his own hole in the sand and had his own well.

This was enough, and more than enough, to restore cheerfulness to the army.

El-Arich surrendered at the first summons.

On the 28th of February, the green and fertile plains of Syria at last became visible in the distance. At the same time, through a light rain—a rare thing in the Orient—one could dimly distinguish mountains and valleys which reminded the beholder of those of Europe.

On the first of March they encamped at Ramlek—the ancient Rama where Rachel yielded to that despair which the Bible describes in those grand lines:

"In Rama there was a voice heard, lamentations and weeping and great mourning; Rachel weeping for her children, and would not be comforted because they were not."

Jesus, the Virgin Mary, and Joseph passed Rama on their way to Egypt, and the church which the monks relinquished to Bonaparte for a hospital was built on the very spot where the Holy Family stopped to rest.

The well whose pure cool water quenched the thirst of the entire army was the same that had quenched the thirst of the holy fugitives seventeen hundred and ninety-nine years before. The disciple Joseph, whose pious hand wrapped the body of our Lord Jesus Christ in his shroud, was likewise from Rama.

Probably not a single man in this vast concourse knew these sacred traditions; but one thing they did know, and that was that they were not more than six leagues from Jerusalem.

As they strolled about under the olive-trees, which are probably the finest in the entire Orient, but which the soldiers remorselessly cut down to make campfires, Bourrienne said to Bonaparte:

"General, will you not go to Jerusalem?"

"Oh, no," he replied carelessly. "Jerusalem is entirely outside of my plan of operations. I have no desire to get into trouble with the mountaineers on these bad roads; besides, on the other side of the mountains I should be attacked by a large body of cavalry. I have no desire to share the fate of Crassus."

Crassus, the reader may recollect, was slain by the Parthians.

It is a strange fact in relation to Bonaparte that though he was within six leagues of Jerusalem (the cradle of Christ) at one time, and within six leagues of Rome, the papal capital, at another, he evinced no desire to see either Rome or Jerusalem.

CHAPTER II

THE PRISONERS

Two days before, when within a quarter of a league of Gaza—which in Arabic signifies "treasure," and in Hebraic "strong,"—that same Gaza whose gates were carried away by Samson, who perished with three thousand Philistines beneath the ruins of the temple he had overthrown—they had met Abdallah, Pasha of Damascus.

He was at the head of his cavalry.

Murat took one hundred men from the thousand under his command, and with his whip in his hand—for he seldom deigned to draw his saber when contending with this Mussulman, Arabian, and Mangrabin cavalry—made a vigorous charge upon them.

Abdallah turned and fled, the French army following him through the town, and taking up its position on the other side.

It was on the day after this skirmish that they reached Ramleh.

From Ramleh they marched upon Jaffa, and to the great delight of the soldiers, the clouds gathered over their heads and rain fell a second time.

A delegation was sent to Bonaparte, asking permission for the army to take a bath.

Bonaparte granted the request, and ordered a halt, so each soldier removed his clothing and allowed the cool rain to fall upon his burning body. Then the army resumed its march, refreshed and cheerful, singing, as if with one voice, the "Marseillaise."

Abdallah's Mamelukes and cavalry were no more willing to wait for the French here than at Gaza, but hastened into the city, firmly convinced that every Mussulman who is behind a rampart is safe.

This garrison at Jaffa which, intoxicated with fanaticism, was about to set at defiance the finest army in the world, was a strange medley, embodying as it did representatives from every part of the Orient—from the furthermost limits of Africa to the furthest extremity of Asia. There were Mangrabins, with their black and white cloaks, and Albanians, with their long guns mounted in silver and incrusted with coral. There were Kurds, with their long lances adorned with bunches of ostrich plumes, and Aleppians, who all wore on one cheek or the other the mark of the famous button of Aleppo. There were men of Damascus, with swords of such finely tempered steel that they would cut a silk handkerchief floating in the air, and there were Natolians, Karamanians, and negroes.

It was the 3d when the army arrived before the gates of Jaffa, and on the 4th the city was invested.

That same day Murat made a reconnaissance around the ramparts, to ascertain where it would be best to make the attack.

On the 7th everything was ready for the bombardment; but before beginning that, Bonaparte concluded to try conciliatory measures, for he knew what a conflict with such a population would be, even if he came off victorious. So he dictated the following summons:

"God is merciful, and compassionate."

"General Bonaparte, whom the Arabs have surnamed the Sultan of Fire, bids me remind you that Djezzar Pasha began hostilities in Egypt by taking the fortress of El-Arich; that God, who is always on the side of the right, gave the victory to the French army, which recaptured the fort. He also bids me inform you that he has come to Palestine to drive out the troops of Djezzar Pasha, who ought never to have entered it; that Jaffa is surrounded on all sides; that the batteries will in two hours proceed to destroy the walls and defenses of the city with shot and shell; that his heart is saddened by the thought of the injury that would befall the city and its inhabitants if it should be taken by assault, and that he consequently offers a safe-conduct to the garrison and protection to the inhabitants of the city, together with a postponement of the bombardment until seven o'clock in the morning."

This communication was addressed to Abou Saib, governor of Jaffa.

Roland extended his hand to take it.

"What do you mean?" asked Bonaparte.

"Don't you want a messenger?" replied the young man, laughing. "I may as well serve in that capacity as anybody else."

"On the contrary, it had much better be some else," replied Bonaparte; "for it must be a Mussulman, not a Christian."

"Why so, General?"

"Because, while Abou Saib *may* cut off the head of a Mussulman, he would be *sure* to cut off the head of a Christian."

"So much the more reason I should go," responded Roland, shrugging his shoulders.

"Enough! I will not permit it," answered Bonaparte.

Roland retreated to a corner, pouting like a spoiled child, and Bonaparte, turning to his dragoman, said:

"See if there is any Turk or Arab, or, in fact, any Mussulman who will undertake to deliver this message."

The dragoman repeated the question in a loud tone, and a Mameluke from the dromedary corps stepped forward.

"I will," he said.

The dragoman glanced inquiringly at Bonaparte.

"Tell him the risk he runs," said the commander-in-chief.

"The Sultan of Fire wishes you to know that you risk your life by undertaking this commission."

"What is written, is written!" answered the Mameluke, holding out his hand.

A trumpeter and a white flag were given to him.

They approached the town on horseback, and the gates opened to admit them.

Ten minutes afterward there was a great commotion on the ramparts directly in front of the general's camp, and the trumpeter appeared, dragged roughly along by two Albanians. They made him sound his trumpet to attract the attention of the French, and he sounded the *diane*.

At that same instant, while all eyes were riveted upon that portion of the wall, a man appeared, holding in his right hand a severed head enveloped in a turban. He stretched his arms over the rampart, the turban slowly unrolled, and the head dropped to the bottom of the wall.

It was the head of the Mussulman who had taken the summons to surrender.

A few minutes afterwards the trumpeter emerged from the same gate through which he had entered, but he was alone.

The next day, at seven o'clock in the morning, six pieces of artillery began to thunder one after another.

By four o'clock the breach was practicable, and Bonaparte ordered the assault. He glanced around for Roland with the intention of giving him command of one of the regiments, but Roland was not there.

The carabineers and chasseurs of the 22d Light Brigade, supported by the artillery, rushed forward under command of General Rambeau, Adjutant General Netherwood, and Vernois.

They all mounted the breach, and in spite of the fierce fusillade that greeted them in front, and the shower of grape from some guns they had not been able to silence, a terrible fight was waged over the remains of the fallen town.

This fight lasted for at least a quarter of an hour without the besiegers being able to force an entrance through the breach or the besieged being able to drive the besiegers back.

All the fighting seemed to be centered at this point, when Roland suddenly appeared upon the dismantled walls waving a Turkish standard and followed by about fifty men.

"The city is taken!" he shouted.

This is what had occurred:

About six o'clock that morning Roland, on going down to the sea to bathe, had discovered a sort of breach at the angle formed by the intersection of one of the walls and a tower: He had first satisfied himself that this breach really led into the city; then he had taken his bath, returning to the camp just as the bombardment began.

There, as he was known to be one of Bonaparte's particular favorites, as well as one of the most daring officers in the army, cries of "Captain Roland! Captain Roland!" resounded on every side.

Roland knew what that meant.

It meant: "Haven't you something of an impossible nature to suggest? Here we are!"

"Fifty volunteers!" he shouted.

One hundred sprung forward.

"Fifty," he repeated, selecting every other man in order not to hurt any person's feelings. Then, taking two drummers and two trumpeters, he himself led the way, through the breach he had discovered, into the city.

His fifty men followed him. They soon met a squad of about one hundred Moslems carrying a flag.

These they quickly dispatched, and Roland took possession of the flag. It was this same flag that he had waved from the wall.

He was greeted with the enthusiastic shouts of the entire

army; but he felt the time had now come to utilize his drums and trumpets.

The entire garrison was at the breach, anticipating no attack elsewhere, when they suddenly heard drums beside them and French trumpets behind them.

At the same time there came two discharges of musketry, and a shower of bullets fell upon the besieged, who turned only to see gun-barrels gleaming and tri-colored plumes waving on every side of them.

The smoke which the sea-breeze blew in upon them concealed the insignificance of the French force from them, and they fancied they had been betrayed. A terrible panic seized them, and they abandoned the breach.

But Roland had already sent ten of his men to open one of the gates, and Lannes' division had poured in through this gateway, so the Mussulmans met French bayonets where they had expected to find the way clear for flight.

With one of those reactions common to ferocious people who, as they never give quarter, expect none in return, they caught up their weapons with increased fury, and the fighting began again.

Bonaparte, ignorant of what was going on in the city, but seeing a dense smoke rising above its walls, and hearing the continuous rattle of musketry, sent Eugene de Beauharnais and Croisier to ascertain the state of affairs..

They both wore upon their arms the scarf of an aid-de-camp, the insignia of their rank, and as they had been waiting with the utmost impatience for a word that would enable them to take part in the fight, they started off at a run, and did not pause until they had reached the very thickest of the fray.

They were recognized as envoys from the commander-in-chief, and as they were supposed to be the bearers of some message, the firing ceased for a moment.

Some of the Albanians could speak French, and one of them cried out:

"We will surrender if you promise that our lives shall be spared. If not, we will fight until the very last one of us is killed."

The two aids-de-camp had no means of knowing Bonaparte's secret wishes. They were both young, and the instincts of humanity were strong in their hearts; so they promised the poor fellows that their lives should be spared, though they had no authority to do so. The firing accordingly ceased, and the prisoners were taken to the French camp.

There were four thousand of them.

As for the soldiers, they knew their rights. The town had been taken by assault, and after the capture came the pillage.

CHAPTER III

THE SLAUGHTER

Bonaparte was pacing to and fro in front of his tent with Bourrienne, impatiently waiting for news, when he saw two large bodies of unarmed men leaving the town by two different gates.

One of them was led by Croisier; the other by Eugene de Beauharnais.

The countenances of both young men were radiant with joy.

Croisier, who had not smiled since he had had the misfortune to offend the commander-in-chief, was smiling now, for he felt confident that this fine prize would bring about a reconciliation between them.

But Bonaparte saw the whole situation at a glance, and turning very pale, he exclaimed, sorrowfully:

"What do they suppose I am going to do with those men? Have I food to give them? Have I vessels in which to send the poor wretches to Egypt or to France?"

The two young men paused a few yards from him. The stern expression of his face told them they had made a terrible mistake.

"What have you there?" he asked.

Croisier dared not reply; so Eugene answered for both:

"Prisoners, as you see, general."

"Did I tell you to take any prisoners?"

"You told us to stop the carnage as much as possible," responded Eugene, timidly.

"Yes, of women and children and aged men, of course, but not of armed soldiers. Do you know that you have made it necessary for me to commit a crime?"

The young men understood him, and shrunk back in dismay. Croisier could not control his feelings, and burst into tears. Eugene tried to console him, but he shook his head despondently, murmuring:

"It's all up with me. I shall allow myself to be shot the first chance I have."

Before deciding the fate of the unfortunate prisoners, Bonaparte concluded to call a council of war, but both soldiers and officers had remained in the city. The soldiers did not cease their deadly work until they became tired of slaughter.

There were five thousand dead, besides the four thousand prisoners.

The pillage continued all night.

Every minute or two shots were heard, and cries of anguish resounded incessantly in the streets, houses, and mosques. They were uttered by Moslem soldiers, who were being dragged from their hiding-places and cruelly slain; by persons who were endeavoring to protect their property; by husbands and fathers who were trying to save their wives or children from the brutality of the soldiers.

But the vengeance of Heaven was concealed under all this cruelty, for the plague was in Jaffa, and the army carried the germs of it away with them.

The prisoners, with their hands tied behind their backs, were all made to sit down together in front of the tents. Their faces were gloomy, rather from a presentiment of what was to come, than anger, however, for they had seen Bonaparte's countenance darken at the sight of them, and had heard, without fully understanding, the reprimand he had bestowed on the two young men.

Some of them ventured to say: "I am hungry;" others, "I am thirsty."

Water was brought to all of them, and each man received a piece of bread taken from the soldiers' rations, and this reassured them somewhat.

As fast as the generals retuned they were requested to step into the tent of the commander-in-chief.

They deliberated there a long time without coming to any decision.

On the following day, when the reports of the generals of division came in, all complained of insufficient rations. The only soldiers who had eaten as much as they wanted were those who had been in the town during the fight and consequently had a right to their share of the plunder.

But these soldiers numbered barely one-fourth of the army, and all the rest grumbled at having to share their rations with enemies who had been rescued from legitimate vengeance, inasmuch as, according to the rules of war, Jaffa, having been taken by storm, all the soldiers within its walls should have perished by the sword.

Another council of war was convened, and five questions were submitted for consideration.

1st. Should the prisoners be sent to Egypt?

To do this a large escort would be required, and the French army was now none too strong to defend itself against the universal and bitter hostility of the country.

Besides, how could the Moslems and their escort be fed until they reached Cairo, traveling through an enemy's country which the French army had just devastated in its passage, when they had no food to give them on their departure?

2d. Should the prisoners be placed on shipboard?

Where were the ships? Where could any be obtained? The sea was deserted, and not a friendly sail was to be seen.

3d. Should they be restored to liberty?

In that case they would either go straight to Saint Jean

d'Acre, to re-enforce the pasha there, or to the mountains of Nabloos, after which the French would be subjected to a constant fusillade from invisible sharp-shooters in every ravine.

4th. Should they be incorporated in the French army?

In that case the supply of provisions, which was already inadequate for ten thousand men, would be even more scanty for fourteen thousand. Besides, such comrades would prove dangerous in a hostile country, and would be almost certain to embrace the first opportunity to give death in exchange for the life which had been spared to them. What is a dog of a Christian to a Turk? Is it not a pious and praiseworthy deed in the eyes of the prophet to kill an infidel?

As the fifth question was about to be submitted, Bonaparte hastily rose.

"Let us wait until to-morrow," he said, though he himself did not know what could possibly be gained by waiting.

It was really for one of those mysterious chances which sometimes prevent the commission of a great crime, and which are styled interpositions of Providence.

But he waited in vain.

On the fourth day, the question which no one had dared to ask the day before, had to be answered.

"Should the prisoners be shot?"

The dissatisfaction was increasing, and the evil itself was growing. The soldiers might throw themselves upon the unfortunate creatures at any moment, and thus give the semblance of revolt and assassination to a measure that was really a necessity.

The decision was unanimous, with one exception.

One of the officers present did not vote at all.

The poor creatures were to be shot.

Bonaparte hurried from his tent and gazed out anxiously over the sea, as if hoping some relief might come from that quarter. A storm of grief and remorse was raging in his heart.

At that time he had not acquired the stoicism subsequently won on numerous battle-fields. This man, who afterward gazed unmoved upon Austerlitz, Eylau, and Moscow, had not yet become sufficiently familiar with death to draw such a prize to him without remorse.

On the vessel that transported him to Egypt, his compassion, like Caesar's, had astonished everybody.

Of course it was inevitable that some accident should occur during so long a voyage, and that a few men should fall into the sea.

This happened several times aboard the "Orient," and as soon as Bonaparte heard a cry of "Man overboard!" he rushed upon deck, if he did not happen to be there already, and ordered a boat lowered. He did not relax his efforts for an instant until the man was found and saved. Bourrienne was ordered to liberally reward all who had aided in the rescue, and if there chanced to be among them any sailor who had incurred punishment for neglect of duty, he forgave the offense, and made him a present of money besides.

One dark night a sound like that of a body falling into the water was heard, and Bonaparte rushed up on deck as usual, and ordered a boat to be lowered.

The sailors, knowing that they would not only be doing a good deed, but that they were sure to be liberally rewarded for it afterward, jumped into the boat without a moment's hesitation. After about five minutes Bonaparte's constantly reiterated question: "Is he saved?—is he saved?" was answered by loud shouts of laughter.

The man that had fallen into the water proved to be a quarter of beef from the store-room.

"Double the reward, Bourrienne," said Bonaparte. "It might have been a man, and the next time they might think it was a quarter of beef."

The order for the execution must come from him. He deferred giving it, and time was passing. At last he called for his horse, sprung into the saddle, took an escort of twenty men, and galloped off, crying:

"Do it!"

He dared not say, "Fire!"

The scene that ensued is one of those that can never be described. The great massacres of ancient times have no counterparts in modern history. Out of the four thousand a few escaped by throwing themselves into the water and swimming to reefs beyond rifle range.

Neither Eugene de Beauharnais nor Croisier dared to enter Bonaparte's presence until they reached Saint Jean d'Acre, and duty obliged them to receive the commander's orders there.

In spite of the English frigates lying at anchor in the harbor, on reaching Saint Jean d'Acre, several of the young men, among them the Sheik of Aher, Roland, and the Comte de Mailly, asked permission to go down to the shore to bathe.

The permission was granted.

While they were diving De Mailly found a leather sack, and the bathers being curious to know what it contained, swam with it to the shore.

It was tied with a strong cord, and seemed to contain a human body.

When the cord was unfastened and the sack emptied on the sand, De Mailly recognized the body and head of his brother, who had been sent with a flag of truce a month before, and whom Djezzar had beheaded on perceiving the cloud of dust raised by the horses of the advance guard of the French army.

CHAPTER IV

FROM ANCIENT TIMES TO OUR OWN DAY

As we are fortunate enough to find readers who are sufficiently intelligent to encourage us to write a book in which romance holds a secondary place, we shall doubtless be excused if we stop long enough to give the ancient as well as the modern history of the places visited by our heroes.

There is a wonderful charm for the philosopher and poet in treading upon soil composed of the ashes of past generations, and the region through which we are now journeying is, above all others, filled to overflowing with traces of those great historical catastrophes which become fainter and fainter in outline with the lapse of time, until they finally disappear like ruins and ghosts of ruins amid the ever-deepening shadows of the past.

This is especially true of the city we have just left filled with shrieks of anguish, its streets flowing with blood, its walls battered to pieces, and its houses in flames.

The swift movement of our story, and our desire to enter modern Jaffa in company with the youthful conqueror, have, up to this time, prevented us from giving even a brief description of the Jaffa of olden times.

Jaffa, in Hebrew, signifies beauty; Joppa, in Phoenician, signifies height.

Jaffa, to the eastern gulf of the Mediterranean, is what Jiddah is to the middle of the Red Sea.

It is pre-eminently a city of pilgrims.

Every Christian pilgrim who goes to Jerusalem to visit the tomb of Christ visits Jaffa *en route*.

Every Mussulman hadji who goes to Mecca to visit Mohammed's grave stops at Jiddah *en route*.

When we read the great books on Egypt—books upon which the greatest savants of the age have united their best efforts—we are amazed to find so few of those luminous points which light and attract the traveler like beacons in the dark night of the past.

We will now attempt to do what they have left undone.

The author who assigns to Jaffa—that is to say, the Joppa of the Phoenicians—the most ancient place in history, is Pomponius Mela, who declares that it was built before the flood.

Est Joppe ante diluvium condita.

And Joppa must have been built before the Deluge, for Josephus, the historian, says, like Berosus and Nicolas of Damascus, not precisely that the ark was built at Joppa—for that would contradict the statements of the Bible—but that it stopped there. They assure us that, even in their day, fragments of it were still shown to incredulous travelers, and that the dust of the tar used in coating the ark was recommended as a universal panacea.

If we believe Pliny, it was at Joppa that Andromeda was chained to the rock to be devoured by the sea-monster, and where she was delivered by Perseus, mounted upon the Chimera and armed with the dread head of Medusa.

He declares, moreover, that in the reign of Adrian the holes through which passed the chain that bound Andromeda could still be seen, and Saint Jerome—a witness who certainly cannot be accused of partiality—declares that he himself saw them.

The skeleton of the sea-monster, forty feet in length, was

believed by the people of Joppa to be that of their goddess Ceto.

The water of the fountain in which Perseus bathed after slaying the monster remained tinged with his blood, and Pausanias tells us he saw the crimsoned water with his own eyes.

This goddess Ceto, to whom Pliny alludes (*colitur fabulosa Ceto*), and who is called Derceto by other historians, was supposed to be the mother of Semiramis.

Didorus of Sicily relates the pretty story of this unknown mother in these words:

"There is," he says, "in Syria a city called Ascalon, which overlooks a large, deep lake in which fish abound, and near which stands a temple dedicated to a celebrated goddess whom the Syrians call Derceto.

"She had the head and face of a woman, but her body was that of a fish. The learned men of the country say that Venus, having become offended with Derceto, inspired her with as intense a passion for a young priest as that which she had inspired in the hearts of Sappho and Phedrus. Derceto had a daughter by him, but repented so bitterly of her fault, that she caused the young man to disappear, abandoned the child to her fate in a lonely place, and threw herself into the lake, where she was changed into a fish. It is on this account the Syrians worship fish as gods, and abstain from eating them.

"But the child was fed by doves, which came in great numbers to build their nests among the rocks where she had been left to die.

"A shepherd afterwards found her, and reared her with as much love and care as if she had been his own child, and he named her Semiramis, or the daughter of the doves."

If we can believe Diodorus, it is to this daughter of the doves, the proud Semiramis, the wife and murderess of Ninus, who fortified Babylon and constructed those magnificent hanging gardens which were the wonder and admiration of the world in ancient times, that the Orientals are indebted for the beautiful costumes which they wear to this day.

When she had reached the zenith of her power, having subjugated Egyptian Arabia, Lybia, a part of Ethiopia, and all Asia as far as the Indus, she felt the necessity of inventing for her long journeys a costume which would not only be convenient and elegant, and in which she could not only perform the ordinary duties of life, but also ride and fight if need be, and this costume was likewise adopted by all the nations she conquered.

"She was so beautiful," says Valerius Maximus, "that one day, an insurrection having broken out while she was at her toilet, she only had to show herself half naked and with hair unbound to restore order at once."

The famous temple of Dagon, where a statue of that god was found overturned and with both hands broken, was in the city of Azoth, between Joppa and Ascalon.

Read the Bible, the masterpiece of history and poesy, and you will see that the cedars of Lebanon used in the construction of Solomon's temple were brought from Joppa. You will see, too, that the prophet Jonah came to Joppa to embark for Tarsus when he was fleeing from the face of the Lord.

Then, passing from the Bible to Josephus, whose history may be truly called a continuation of it, you will see that Judas Maccabaeus, to avenge the death of two hundred of his brethren, who had been slain by the inhabitants of Joppa, came with a sword in one hand and a torch in the other, and set fire to the ships in the harbor, and put to the sword all who escaped the fire.

We read too in the Acts of the Apostles:

"Now there was at Joppa a certain disciple named Tabitha, which by interpretation is called Dorcas; this woman was full of good works and alms deeds which she did.

"And it came to pass in those days that she was sick and

died; whom when they had washed, they laid her in an upper chamber.

"And for as much as Lydda was nigh to Joppa, and the disciples had heard that Peter was there; they sent unto him two men, desiring him that he would not delay to come to them.

"Then Peter arose and went with them. When he was come, they brought him into the upper chamber; and all the widows stood by him weeping, and showing the coats and garments which Dorcas made while she was with them.

"But Peter put them all forth, and kneeled down and prayed; and turning him to the body, said, 'Tabitha, arise!' And she opened her eyes; and when she saw Peter she sat up.

"And he gave her his hand and lifted her up, and when he had called the saints and widows, presented her alive.

"And it was known throughout all Joppa, and many believed in the Lord.

"And it came to pass that he tarried many days in Joppa, with one Simon, a tanner."

It was there that the servants of the centurion Cornelius found him when they came to ask him to go to Caesarea. It was in Simon's house that he had the vision commanding him to preach the gospel to the Gentiles.

At the time of the Jewish revolts against Rome Sextus besieged Joppa, took it by storm, and burned it.

Eight thousand of the inhabitants perished; but it was soon rebuilt. As the new city was constantly sending out pirates who infested the coasts of Syria, and extended their depredations to Greece, and even Egypt, the Emperor Vespasian took it again, razed it to the ground, and built a fortress upon the site; but in his history of the Jewish wars, Josephus relates that a new city soon sprung up at the foot of the fortress, a city which was the seat of a bishopric from the reign of Constantine, A. D. 330, until the invasion of the Arabs in 636.

This bishopric was established during the First Crusade;

but was finally converted into a countship, and embellished and fortified by Baldwin I., Emperor of Constantinople.

Saint Louis likewise paid a visit to Jaffa, and Joinville, his artless historian, speaks of his extended sojourn there with the Comte de Japhe, as the worthy chevalier styles him.

This Comte de Japhe was Gautier de Brienne, who exerted himself to the uttermost to clean and whitewash his town, which was in such a pitiable condition that Saint Louis was ashamed of it, and took it upon himself to rebuild the walls and beautify the churches.

It was while he was in Joppa that Saint Louis received the news of his mother's death.

"When the saintly king," says Joinville, "saw the Archbishop of Tyre and his confessor enter his apartments with an expression of profound grief upon their countenances, he asked them to accompany him to his chapel, which was his refuge from the sorrows of the world.

"Then when he heard the fatal news, he fell upon his knees, and, clasping his hands, exclaimed:

"'I thank Thee, O God, that Thou didst lend my mother to me for a season, and that Thou now; in Thy good pleasure, hast taken her to Thyself again, it is true that I loved her above all other creatures, and she deserved it; but as Thou hast taken her from me, may Thy name be blessed for evermore.'"

The buildings erected by Saint Louis were destroyed in 1268 by Bibas, Pasha of Egypt, who leveled the citadel to the ground, and sent the wood and marble of which it was composed to Cairo to be used in the erection of a mosque.

So when Monconys visited Palestine he found only a castle and three caves hollowed out of the rock at Jaffa.

We have described the condition in which Bonaparte left it. We shall return again to this town, which, to Bonaparte, was neither Jaffa the Beautiful, nor Joppa the Lofty; but Jaffa the Fatal.

CHAPTER V

SIDNEY SMITH

At daybreak on the morning of the 18th, while the army was crossing the little river called the Kerdaneah, on a bridge constructed during the previous night, Bonaparte, accompanied by Roland de Montrevel, the Sheik of Aher, and the Comte de Mailly, whom all the commander-in-chief's efforts had been powerless to console for the loss of his brother, ascended a small hill only a short distance from the town to which he had just laid siege.

From the summit of this hill he had an extended view of the whole surrounding country, including not only the two English war-ships "Tiger" and "Thesus" swinging at anchor, but the gardens around the city filled with the pasha's troops.

"Have those miscreants dislodged and driven back into the town!" he exclaimed.

As he addressed this order to no particular person, all three men started off together, like so many hawks in pursuit of the same prey.

But in a harsh voice he cried:

"Roland! Sheik of Aher!"

These two young men, on hearing their names, stopped their horses and returned to their places be side the commander-in-chief, while De Mailly, with one hundred sharp shooters and the same number of grenadiers and voltigeurs, urged his horse into a gallop and charged at their head.

Bonaparte was a great believer in omens, and it was for this reason that he had been so incensed by Croisier's hesitation during their first engagement with the Bedouins, and that he had reproved him so sharply for it.

Through his fine field-glass he could see the movements of the troops distinctly from where he stood. He saw Eugene de Beauharnais and Croisier—who had not ventured to speak to him since the affair at Jaffa—assume command, the former of the grenadiers and the latter of the sharp-shooters, while De Mailly headed the voltigeurs.

While Roland was nervously gnawing the silver handle of his riding-whip, and the Sheik of Aher, on the contrary, was watching the fight with all the composure of a true Arab, Bonaparte saw the three detachments dash through the ruins of a village, a Turkish cemetery, and a small strip of woods, and hurl themselves upon the enemy, in spite of a brisk fusillade from the Arnauts and Albanians, whom he could distinguish by their magnificent gold-embroidered garments and their long, silver-mounted rifles, and rout them at the first charge.

The firing of the French continued with steadily increasing vigor, while above it could be heard the loud explosions of the hand-grenades which our soldiers hurled at the fugitives.

Pursuers and pursued reached the wall of the city almost at the same time; but the posterns being closed behind the Mussulmans, and the ramparts being encircled by a girdle of fire, the three hundred Frenchmen were obliged to beat a retreat, after having killed about one hundred and fifty of the enemy.

The three youthful leaders displayed wonderful bravery, and really performed prodigies of valor in emulation of one another.

Eugene had killed an Arnaut a head taller than himself in a hand-to-hand struggle; De Mailly, who had approached within a few yards of a group that was making a stand, fired both his pistols at them and rejoined his men with a single bound, and Croisier had slain two Arabs who made an attack upon him simultaneously, cleaving the skull of the first and breaking off the blade of his saber in the breast of the second.

Bonaparte turned to the Sheik of Aher.

"Give me your sword in exchange for mine," he said; and detaching his own sword from his belt, he handed it to the sheik.

The latter kissed the handle, rapturously and handed the general his own in return.

"Roland," said Bonaparte, "go and present my compliments to De Mailly and Eugene. As for Croisier, you will merely hand him this sword, and say: 'Here is a sword the commander-in-chief sends you. He has been watching you.'"

Roland started off at a gallop.

The young men to whom the general had sent his congratulations fairly leaped in their saddles, so great was their delight.

Croisier like the Sheik of Aher, kissed the sword which had been presented to him, threw away the broken hilt and scabbard of the old one, and placed the one Bonaparte had given him in his belt, saying:

"Thank the commander-in-chief for me, and tell him he will have good reason to be content with me at the first assault."

The entire French army had now ascended the hill, where Bonaparte was standing like an equestrian statue, and the men uttered shouts of delight when they saw their comrades driving the Mangrabins before them as the wind drives the sand of the desert. Like Bonaparte, the French soldiers saw very little difference between the fortifications of Saint Jean d'Acre and those of Joppa, and, like Bonaparte, they did not doubt for one instant that the city would be taken at the second or third assault.

The French were not aware that there were then in Saint Jean d'Acre two men who were worth far more than an entire army of Mussulmans—Sidney Smith, the English admiral who commanded the "Tiger" and "Thesus," which were riding at anchor in the Gulf of Carmel, and Colonel Phélippeaux, who had charge of the defenses and fortress of Djezzar the Butcher.

Strange to say, Phélippeaux had been the friend and schoolmate of Bonaparte at Brienne, a formidable rival too at college and in his mathematical successes, though chance or accident had now placed him among the young general's foes.

Sidney Smith, whom the exiles of the 18th Fructidor had met in the Temple, had, by a strange freak of fortune, escaped from his prison, reached London in safety, and resumed his place in the English navy about the time of Bonaparte's departure from Toulon.

It was Phélippeaux who had planned the escape of Sidney Smith, and who had succeeded in his dangerous undertaking. Forged orders had been presented for the ostensible object of removing the captive to another prison. A facsimile of the signature of the minister of police had been secured at great cost. From whom? From the minister himself, perhaps; who knows? Under the name of Loger, and in the uniform of an adjutant general, Sidney Smith's friend presented himself at the prison and displayed the order to the clerk, who examined it carefully, and was obliged to admit that it was perfectly *en regle* in every respect.

Nevertheless, he said:

"For such an important prisoner you will need a guard of at least six men."

Whereupon the pretended adjutant replied:

"For a prisoner of such importance his word is all that is necessary."

Then, turning to the prisoner, he added:

"Commodore, you are a military man, and so am I. Your

word of honor that you will not attempt to escape will satisfy me. If you will give me that I shall need no escort."

And Sidney Smith, who, like the honorable Englishman that he was, would not utter a lie even to insure his escape, had answered:

"If this assurance will satisfy you, monsieur, I will swear to accompany you wherever you go."

And Sir Sidney Smith accompanied Adjutant General Loger to England.

And these two men were now let loose upon Bonaparte.

Phélippeaux was intrusted with the defense of the fortress, as we have said, and Sidney Smith with providing arms and soldiers.

So where Bonaparte expected to find only a stupid Turkish officer in command as at Gaza and Joppa, he had to contend with all the skill of a compatriot and all the animosity of an Englishman.

That same evening Bonaparte ordered Sanson, the chief of the engineer corps, to examine the counterscarp.

There was no moon; so the night was well adapted to such an operation, and Sanson waited until it became very dark. Then he set out alone, traversed the ruins of the village, the cemetery, and the gardens, from which the Arabs had been dislodged and driven into the town that morning. At last, seeing a huge mass of even denser darkness in front of him, and knowing it could be nothing else than the fortress, he got down on his hands and knees and began to feel his ground inch by inch. Just as he came to a much steeper incline, which convinced him that the moat was entirely destitute of facing, he was seen by a sentinel, whose eyes were either more accustomed to the darkness or who possessed that faculty of seeing distinctly at night which seems to characterize some men as well as some animals, and the cry of, "Who goes there?" suddenly rang out upon the air.

Sanson made no reply. The cry was repeated a second

and even a third time. A shot followed, and a bullet shattered the outstretched hand of the chief of the engineer corps.

In spite of the terrible pain, the officer did not utter a sound, but crawled back to report to Bonaparte.

The next day the trench was begun; but ignorant of the valuable coadjutors Djezzar Pasha possessed, the French made their trench barely three feet deep, and the gigantic Kléber, on seeing it, shrugged his shoulders, and exclaimed:

"A fine trench, truly, general! It doesn't reach up to my knees."

On the 23d of March Sidney Smith captured two vessels which were bringing the heavy artillery as well as supplies, and as the French looked on helplessly, they saw themselves in the strange position of besiegers who were being worsted with their own weapons.

On the 25th they made a breach in the wall, and attempted an assault, but were checked in their advance by a counterscarp and a ditch.

On the 26th the besieged, commanded by Djezzar in person, made a sortie for the purpose of destroying the works which had been begun; but a vigorous bayonet charge drove them back, and compelled them to again seek shelter within the walls.

The French artillery consisted only of four twelve-pounders, eight eight-pounders, and four howitzers. These opened fire on the 28th, and though Djezzar's guns were of much heavier caliber than ours, they were soon silenced, and by three o'clock in the afternoon they had not only been silenced but a practicable breach had been made in the tower.

When they saw the wall crumbling and daylight streaming through from the other side, a deafening cheer burst from the French army, and the grenadiers who had been the first to enter Jaffa, confident that it would be equally easy to take Acre, begged to be permitted to storm the breach.

Bonaparte, though he had been in the trench since morning with his staff, hesitated to give the order for the assault, but urged by De Mailly, who came to tell him that he could not possibly restrain the grenadiers any longer, Bonaparte reluctantly consented.

The grenadiers of the Sixty-Ninth Brigade, led by De Mailly, dashed forward; but to their great astonishment, they found an escarpment at least twelve feet high where they had expected to find the sloping sides of the moat.

They called loudly for ladders, which were quickly thrown to them, and De Mailly, seizing the first ladder, lifted it to the breach, where twenty others were soon ranged beside it.

But the breach was now filled with Arnauts and Albanians, who fired full in the faces of their opponents, rolling the very stones from the walls down upon their assailants. In another moment half the ladders were broken in twain, carrying down with them in their fall the persons who chanced to be upon them. De Mailly, who was wounded, fell from the top to the bottom of his.

The firing of the Moslems increased in fury, and the grenadiers were obliged to beat a hasty retreat and to use for mounting the counterscarp the ladders they had expected to use in scaling the breach.

De Mailly, who was wounded in the foot, and who could not walk, begged his men to take him away with them.

One of the men took him on his shoulders, carried him about ten feet, and fell shot through the head.

A second grenadier picked up the wounded man, and carried him to the foot of the ladder, but fell there with his thigh broken. Eager to insure their own safety, the soldiers deserted their leader, though they could hear him crying out:

"At least put an end to me with a bullet if you cannot save me!"

Poor De Mailly did not have long to suffer, however. The moat was no sooner deserted by the French soldiers than the Turks leaped down and cut off the heads of all the wounded that remained there.

Djezzar, thinking to bestow an acceptable gift upon Sidney Smith, had all these heads put into a sack and taken to the English commander.

But Smith shuddered as he looked at this ghastly trophy, and murmured:

"This is what comes of being allied with barbarians!"

CHAPTER VI

PTOLEMAIS

However indifferent Bonaparte may have seemed in relation to Jerusalem, having passed within six leagues of it without stopping to visit it, he was none the less interested in the history of the ground upon which he stood. Not having been able, or not having cared, to do like Alexander, who, after the conquest of India, went considerably out of his way to visit the high priest at Jerusalem, he felt that it was some compensation to stand upon the site of ancient Ptolemais, and to pitch his tent where Richard Coeur de Lion and Philip Augustus had pitched theirs.

In fact, he was not a little elated by his historical surroundings, and he had selected for his headquarters the slight eminence from which he had watched the fight the first day, confident that the famous warriors who had preceded him must have established theirs on the same spot, and on the very evening following the unsuccessful assault in which poor De Mailly perished, he assembled his generals in his tent, and ordered Bourrienne to take from his boxes the few volumes that composed his library.

Unfortunately, it contained very few historical works that treated of Syria. He had only Plutarch, the lives of Cicero, Pompey, Alexander, and Antony, the Old and New Testaments, and a book on mythology. These volumes and the historical knowledge of the more literary of his officers furnishing the only information he could obtain, the sources of his information were necessarily very incomplete.

We who are more favored, inasmuch as we have the history of the Crusades to refer to, are able to lift the veil for our readers, and tell them the history of this corner of the earth from the day on which it fell to the portion of the tribe of Asher, at the time of the division of the Promised Land, until the day when a second Coeur de Lion attempted to wrest it from the Saracens for the third time.

Its ancient name was Acco, signifying "burning sand," and the Arabs still call it Acca; but made tributary to Egypt by the sovereigns of the Greek dynasty of Ptolemy, who inherited Alexandria at the demise of the great conqueror of India, it took the name of Ptolemais about one hundred and six years before Christ.

Vespasian spent three months at Ptolemais while fitting out his expedition against Judea, and held his court there for all the kings and princes of the surrounding countries.

It was there, too, that Titus first saw Berenice, the daughter of Agrippa I., and fell in love with her. But the only work Bonaparte possessed treating upon this period was Racine's tragedy which he was so fond of hearing Talma recite.

In the Acts of the Apostles, you recollect, Saint Paul says:

"From Tyre we came to Ptolemais, where our voyage ended, and having saluted the brethren, we abode one day with them."

The Crusaders first laid siege to Ptolemais in 1189. Boah-Eddin, an Arabian historian, speaking of the Christians, says they were so numerous that God alone could number them; but on the other hand, Gauthier Vinisauf, a Christian writer, assures us that the army of Saladin greatly outnumbered that of Darius.

After the battle of Tiberias—to which we shall have occasion to refer in our description of the battle of Mount

Tabor, Guy de Lusignan, who had escaped from captivity and come to lay siege to Jerusalem—the fortifications of Saint Jean d'Acre had just been rebuilt and strengthened by two immense towers on the side next the sea.

One was called the Tower of Flies, because, being the place where the pagans offered up their sacrifices, the flies were attracted by the flesh of the victims, and the other the Accursed Tower, because, as Gauthier Vinisauf says in his "History of King Richard," it was in this tower that the thirty pieces of silver for which Judas betrayed our Saviour were struck off.

It was by this very same Accursed Tower that, in 1291, the Saracens forced their way into the city and took it, and although he was ignorant of the fact, it was upon this very same tower that Bonaparte had just made his unsuccessful attack.

Walter Scott, in one of his best romances, "The Talisman," relates an incident of this famous siege, which lasted two years, and several Arabian histories contain some very interesting particulars in regard to it.

Ibn-Alatir, Saladin's physician, has left us a very interesting description of the Moslem camp.

"In the middle of this camp," he says, "was an immense square, in which the forges of the farriers had been set up. There were one hundred and forty of them. We can judge of the magnitude of the camp from that fact.

"In a single kitchen there were twenty-nine pots, each large enough to hold a large sheep. I myself counted the number of shops registered by the inspector of markets. There were seven thousand of them, and you must understand that they were not like our city shops. A single camp shop would make a hundred like ours, and all were well stocked. I heard it said that when Saladin moved his camp to Karouba it cost one butter merchant seventy pieces of gold to move his stock, though the distance was so short.

"As for the shops for the sale of clothing, they were beyond computation; and there were over a thousand bathing establishments in the camp. They were kept by Africans, and it cost a piece of silver to take a bath."

The camp of the Christians was exactly like a fortified city, every European art and trade having its representatives there. The markets were as abundantly supplied with meat, fish, and fruit as those of the capital of any great nation would have been. There were even churches with bells; so it was usually at the hour for mass that the Saracens attacked the camp.

"A poor English priest built at his own expense," says Michaud, "a chapel consecrated to the dead upon the plains of Ptolemais. There was a large cemetery of consecrated ground around this chapel, and chanting the office for the dead, he himself followed thither the mortal remains of more than one hundred thousand pilgrims. Forty lords of Bremen and Lubeck made tents from the sails of their vessels to shelter the sick soldiers of their nation, and this was the origin of the celebrated organization which still exists under the name of the 'Teutonic Order.'"

Every person who has traveled in Egypt or the East, or who has visited Constantinople, has made the acquaintance of the wonderful Turkish Punchinello called Caragous, beside whom the exploits of our own Punchinello fade into insignificance.

It was during this siege in which Richard Coeur de Lion, Philip Augustus, and Saladin played such important parts that the ancestors of the modern Caragous first made its appearance.

He was an emir.

Another very important date to verify is that of the first bill of exchange. Emad Eddin speaks of an envoy from the Caliph of Bagdad who was the bearer of two cargoes of naphtha and reeds, and who also brought with him five persons skilled in the distillation and use of naphtha. It was a well-known fact that naphtha and Greek fire are one and the same thing.

Furthermore, this same embassador brought a note of hand for twenty thousand pieces of gold on the merchants of Bagdad, so the bill of exchange and the note of hand are not inventions of modern commerce, as they were used in the East as early as the year 1191.

It was also during this long siege that the Moslems invented the *zenbourech*, which the popes subsequently forbid the Christians to use.

It was a sort of gigantic arrow, thirty centimeters long and twelve thick. It was four-sided, had an iron point, and a head ornamented with feathers.

Vinisauf states that this terrible weapon, hurled with great force by the machine used to impel it, would sometimes pass through the bodies of two men armed with shields, and then bury itself in the wall.

It was near the close of this siege that the famous quarrel occurred that estranged Richard of England and Leopold, Duke of Austria.

Richard, who often returned from an assault—at least so his historian says—so riddled with arrows pins, was justly proud of his strength and courage.

Leopold, who was also exceedingly brave, ordered his flag to be hoisted over one of the towers of the city which he had entered with Richard. Richard might have placed his own flag beside that of Duke Leopold; but instead of doing that, he chose to pull down the Austrian flag and throw it into a ditch. All the Germans became furiously angry, and begged to be allowed to make an attack upon the king in his camp, but Leopold would not permit this.

A year afterward, as Richard did not think it advisable to return to England by way of France, on account of his difference with Philip Augustus, he attempted to travel through Austria in disguise, but was recognized in spite of it, made a prisoner, and confined in the Castle of Durenstein. For two years no one had any idea what had become of him. This god of war seemed to have vanished as suddenly and as completely as a meteor.

But a nobleman of Arras, named Blondel, started out to find him, and one day, without the slightest suspicion that he was so near the English king, he sat down at the foot of the wall of an old castle, and happened to sing the first couplet of a ballad which he and the king had composed together, for Richard condescended to write a bit of poetry now and then in his leisure moments.

Now, the king happened to be imprisoned in this very castle, and as soon as he heard the first lines of the song he suspected Blondel must be near, and responded by singing the second stanza; and the rest of the episode which furnished Gretel with the theme for a *chef d'oeuvre* is known to every one.

Ptolemais surrendered to the Christians, as we have said, after a two years' siege, and the garrison were promised their lives on condition that they would restore the True Cross, which had been captured at the battle of Tiberius; but it is needless to say that as soon as the Saracens were restored to liberty they forgot all about their promise.

One hundred years afterward Ptolemais was retaken from the Christians, never to be surrendered to them again.

This siege, too, had its strange chroniclers and its vicissitudes that stirred all Europe, as well as many deeds characterized by marvelous courage and self-abnegation.

Saint Antonius cites one strange instance of this.

"There was," he says, "at Saint Jean d'Acre a well-known convent belonging to the order of Saint Claire. When the Saracens entered the town, the abbess had the convent-bell rung, and the entire sisterhood collected together. Then addressing the nuns, she said:

"'My dear daughters and well-beloved sisters, you have promised our Lord Jesus Christ to be His spotless wives. We are now exposed to a two-fold peril—our purity and our lives are both in danger. The enemies of our souls, and of our bodies as well, are near at hand—enemies who, after dishonoring those they meet, put them to the sword. Though we cannot escape them by flight, we can do so by making a painful but determined resolve. It is a woman's beauty that oftenest attracts men; so let us despoil ourselves of all attractions. Let us use our faces as a means of preserving our spiritual beauty and our chastity intact. I will set you the example, and then let all who desire to present themselves spotless before their spotless Bridegroom follow my example.'

"And having said this, she cut off her nose with a razor. The others followed her example, and courageously disfigured themselves in order that they might appear more beautiful in the eyes of Christ.

"In this way they preserved their purity, for the Moslems," continues Saint Antonius, "seeing their bleeding faces, were filled with horror and loathing, and contented themselves with taking their lives."

CHAPTER VII

THE SCOUTS

On the same night that Bonaparte assembled his staff, not for a council of war, but as a sort of literary and historical society, several messengers came to the Sheik of Aher to report that an army, under the Pasha of Damascus, was about to cross the Jordan in order to compel Bonaparte to abandon the siege of Saint Jean d'Acre.

This army, which consisted of nearly twenty-five thousand men—according to the always exaggerated acounts of the Arabs—had an immense provision train with it, and was to cross the Jordan at Jacob's Bridge.

Djezzar's emissaries had also been all along the coast of Said, and the contingent of that region had joined that of Aleppo and Damascus with the greater feeling of security, for the reason that the pasha's agents had circulated the report everywhere that the French army consisted of only a handful of men, that they had no artillery, and that it would only be necessary for the Pasha of Damascus to unite with Djezzar to entirely exterminate Bonaparte and his army.

On hearing this news, Bonaparte threw down the volume of Plutarch he had been reading, and summoned Junot, Vial, and Murat. He sent Vial northward to take possession of Tyre, Murat eastward to ensure the safety of Fort Zaphet, and Junot southward, with orders to take possession of Nazareth.

Vial crossed the mountains of Cape Blanc, and on the 3d of April came in sight of Tyre. From a slight eminence near the village the French general could see the terrified inhabitants fleeing in confusion; so soon afterward he entered the town without the slightest opposition, promised protection to the people that had remained, persuaded them to go and look for those who had run away, and after two or three days had the satisfaction of seeing them all back in their homes once more.

On the 6th of April, Vial returned to Saint Jean d'Acre, leaving a garrison of two hundred men at Tyre.

Murat had been equally fortunate in his undertaking. A few shots had driven away half the garrison at Fort Zaphet, after which the others, mostly Mangrabins, had offered to place themselves under Murat's orders. From this point he had gone on to the Jordan, reconnoitered its right bank, taken a look at the Lake of Tiberias, then leaving a well-provisioned French garrison in the fort, had likewise returned on the 6th of April in company with his Mangrabins.

Junot had taken Nazareth, our Saviour's birthplace, and had encamped there, partly within and partly outside the village, waiting for further orders from Bonaparte, who told him not to return until he was sent for.

But all Murat's attempts to reassure the commander-in-chief proved futile. His presentiments, together with the persistency of the Sheik of Aher, made him very uneasy about this invisible army that was said to be marching against him; so he gladly accepted the sheik's offer to go as a scout to the shores of Lake Tiberias.

Roland, who was tired of remaining in camp, asked permission to accompany the sheik on his exploring expedition, and that very night they set out, taking advantage of the coolness and darkness to make their way to the plain of Esdrelon, which afforded them the shelter of the mountains of Nabloos on the right and those of Nazareth on the left.

On the 7th of April, 1799, the promontory on which

Saint Jean d'Acre—the Ptolemais of ancient times—stands, was enveloped in as much thunder and lightning as Mount Sinai on the day the Lord issued the law to Moses from the burning bush.

Whence came these deafening reverberations that shook the coast of Syria as if by an earthquake?

Whence came this smoke that covered the Gulf of Carmel with a cloud as thick as if Mount Elias had been suddenly transformed into a volcano?

We began the first chapter of this new narrative in this way. The other chapters have only served to explain the events that preceded this Syrian campaign, which might be truly styled the Eighth, and probably the last, Crusade.

Bonaparte was about beginning his second attack upon the place, having taken advantage of the return of Murat and Vial to try his fortune again.

He was in the trench only about one hundred feet from the ramparts. Beside him stood General Caffarelli, with whom he was talking. That officer was standing with his hand on his hip to assist him in balancing himself on his wooden leg, and his elbow joint projected a trifle above the wall of the trench.

The top of Bonaparte's three-cornered hat was also visible. A bullet suddenly knocked it from his head. He stooped to pick it up, and noticing the general's position as he did so, he stepped a little closer to him, and said:

"General, these Arnauts and Albanians are excellent marksmen, as my hat shows. Take care that they don't serve your arm as they did my hat."

Caffarelli made a disdainful movement.

The gallant general had left one of his legs on the banks of the Rhine, and did not seem to be at all worried at the idea of leaving some other part of his body on the banks of the Kerdaneah, for he did not move.

But a moment later Bonaparte saw him start and turn with his arm hanging shattered at his side.

A bullet had struck his elbow, breaking the joint.

At the same time Bonaparte looked up and saw Croisier standing on the edge of the trench a short distance from him. It was a piece of senseless bravado, and Bonaparte called out:

"Come down, Croisier! You have no business there. Come down, I say!"

"Didn't you say in public one day that I was a coward?" asked the young man.

"I was wrong, Croisier," replied the general. "You have convinced me since then that I was mistaken. Come down!"

Croisier started to obey; but he fell down instead.

A bullet had broken his thigh.

"Larrey, Larrey, come here!" cried Bonaparte, stamping his foot impatiently. "Here is some work for you!"

Larrey hastened up. They laid Croisier on some muskets and carried him from the trench. As for Caffarelli, he walked away, leaning on the arm of the surgeon.

Now let us leave this siege—resumed under such gloomy auspices—to take its course, and cast a glance at the flower decked plain of Esdrelon and the river Kishon, whose course is marked by a long line of rose laurels.

Two horsemen were riding along the bank of this stream. One, dressed in the green uniform of the mounted chasseurs, with his saber at his side, and a three-cornered hat on his head, was fanning himself with his handkerchief.

The other wore a red turban fastened around his head by a band of chamois skin. A head-dress of brilliant colors drooped from the sides and back of his head down upon his shoulders. His form was completely enveloped in a white cashmere burnous, which, when it opened, revealed a rich caftan of green velvet embroidered with gold. His sash was of varied colors, which blended with that marvelous taste found only in Eastern fabrics. Two silver-mounted pistols, with handles of wonderfully beautiful filigree work, were stuck in one side of this sash. His sword alone was of

French make. He wore full red satin trousers, stuck in green leggings embroidered like the caftan, and of the same material, and he held in his hand a long slender lance, light as a reed but strong as a bar of iron, tipped at the end with a bunch of ostrich feathers.

The two young men paused in the shade of a small grove of palms at a bend in the stream and chatting pleasantly together, as befitted traveling companions, began to prepare their breakfast, which consisted of a few pieces of biscuit which the young Frenchman took from his holsters and dipped in the river for a moment.

As for the Arab, he began to look around and above him; then, without uttering a word, attacked with his sword one of the palms, whose tender wood yielded readily to the sharp steel.

"This is certainly a fine sword the commander-in-chief gave me a few days ago," he remarked. "I hope to try it upon something besides palm-trees before long."

"I should say so," replied the Frenchman, crushing a biscuit between his teeth. "It is an article of Versailles manufacture. But are you destroying that poor tree merely to test your new weapon?"

"Look!" said the Arab, pointing upward.

"Ah! I see; it is a date-palm, and we shall have a better breakfast than I thought."

Just then the tree fell with a crash, bringing down with it quite enough fully ripe dates for two or three meals.

They attacked the manna the Lord had provided with all the zest of twenty-five year appetites, and were in the middle of their meal when the Arab's horse began to neigh.

Uttering an exclamation of surprise, the sheik darted out of the grove, and shading his eyes with his hand, eagerly scrutinized the plain.

"What is it?" asked the French man, carelessly.

"One of my tribe mounted on a fine mare. We shall probably learn from him all we need to know."

He returned and reseated himself beside his companion without troubling himself about his horse, which had started off at a gallop to meet the advancing steed.

A few minutes later the gallop of two horses was heard, and a Druse, who had recognized his chief's horse, paused near the grove of palms where another horse indicated that a party had halted, even though there were no other signs of an encampment.

"Azib," cried the Arab chief.

The Druse leaped from his horse and advanced toward the sheik, with his hands crossed upon his breast and bowing low. The sheik exchanged a few words with him in Arabic.

"I was right," remarked the sheik, turning to his companion. "The pasha's advanced guard has just crossed Jacob's Bridge."

"We will go and see for ourselves," replied Roland, whom our readers have doubtless already recognized by his indifference to danger.

"There is no need. Azib has seen," replied the sheik.

"Yes, but perhaps Azib did not see correctly," responded Roland. "I shall feel much better satisfied if I see for myself. That big mountain before us must be Mount Tabor. The Jordan, consequently, is just beyond. We cannot be more than a quarter of a league from it. Let us go and look, and then we shall know exactly what to depend upon."

And without troubling himself to see whether the sheik and Azib intended to follow him or not, Roland sprung upon his horse, which, refreshed by the halt they had made, galloped swiftly off in the direction of Mount Tabor.

A moment afterward he heard his two companions galloping up behind him.

CHAPTER VIII

THE BEAUTIFUL DAUGHTERS OF NAZARETH

He rode for nearly a league over this magnificent plain of Esdrelon—the largest and most celebrated in all Palestine, except that of the Jordan.

In ancient times it was called the paradise and granary of Syria, the plain of Jezreel, the field of Esdrela, the plain of Mejiddo. It figures under all these names in the Bible. It witnessed the defeat of the Midianites and the Amalekites by Gideon. It beheld Saul encamped by the fountain of Jezreel to fight the Philistines assembled at Aphik. It saw Saul, when ruin overtook him, throw himself upon his sword, and saw his three sons perish with him.

It was upon this plain that poor Naboth had his vineyard, near Ahab's palace, and that the infamous Jezebel had him stoned to death as a blasphemer in order to secure possession of his property. It was here that Joram had his heart pierced by an arrow thrown by the hand of Jehu; and finally it was almost on the very spot where the young men had breakfasted that Jezebel was thrown from a window by order of Jehu, and her body devoured by dogs.

In mediaeval times this plain which had witnessed so many tragedies was known as the plain of Sabas. Now it is called "Merdj ibn Amer," which signifies Pastures of the Sons of Amer. It extends between the mountains of Gilboa and those of Nazareth for about five leagues.

At the further end of it rises Mount Tabor, toward which the three riders were galloping, without giving a thought to the celebrity of the ground which they were traversing.

Mount Tabor is easily accessible on all sides, and particularly so on the side next Fouli—that by which they were approaching.

They were obliged to ascend to its summit—an easy task for their Arab horses—before they could see over the two small hills which obstructed the view of the Jordan and Lake Tiberias from any less elevated point.

In proportion as they ascended the mountain the horizon broadened before them, and soon they saw lying before them, like a broad expanse of bright blue satin framed with golden sand on one side and tawny foot-hills on the other, the Lake of Tiberias, connected with the Dead Sea by the Jordan, which winds in and out across the barren plain like a golden ribbon sparkling in the sunlight, and then they discerned the pasha's army slowly advancing up the eastern shore of the lake and crossing the Jordan at Jacob's Bridge, the whole of the advanced guard having already disappeared between the mountain and the Lake of Tiberias.

It was impossible for the beholder to form even an approximate estimate of the size of this vast army.

The cavalry alone covered leagues of ground, and although the young men were four leagues away, they could see weapons glittering in the sunlight, and flashes of gold seemed to dart from the clouds of dust raised by the horses' feet.

It was then about three o'clock in the afternoon, so there was no time to lose. By resting an hour or two by the river Kishon, the Sheik of Aher and Azib could reach Bonaparte's camp about daybreak and warn him.

As for Roland, he announced that he would go to Nazareth and put Junot on his guard, intending all the while to remain and fight with him there, where he could enjoy more freedom of action.

The three young men hastily descended the mountain. At its base they separated, the two Arabs riding straight down the plain, Roland spurring straight for Nazareth, whose white dwellings he had seen from the top of the mountain lying like a nest of doves amid the dark verdure.

Any person who has ever visited Nazareth will remember the abominable roads leading to it. Now on the right, now on the left, the road is edged with precipices, and the beautiful flowers that spring up wherever there is soil enough for them to take root add much to the pleasure of the journey, though they make it no less dangerous. There are snowy lilies, yellow narcissi, sky-blue crocuses, and a profusion of roses of indescribable freshness and sweetness. Does not the Hebrew word *nezer*, the root of Nazareth, signify "flower"?

Owing to the many windings of the road, Roland had several glimpses of Nazareth before he reached it. When he was within about ten minutes' ride of the town, he met a detachment of grenadiers belonging to the Nineteenth Brigade, and telling them who he was, he inquired whether the general was in Nazareth or somewhere in its environs.

The general was at Nazareth, having returned from visiting the outposts only a quarter of an hour before.

Roland was obliged to let his horse walk now, for the noble animal had just traveled eighteen or twenty leagues without any rest save that which their brief halt for breakfast had afforded, but as Roland was now sure of finding the general, there was no especial haste.

On entering the village he met a squad of dragoons in command of Major Desnoyers, one of his friends, and intrusting his horse to the care of a soldier, he asked the way to General Junot's quarters.

It was now about half-past five in the afternoon, and glancing at the sun, which was just disappearing behind the mountains of Nabloos, Desnoyers laughingly replied:

"This is the time when the women of Nazareth go to the

spring for water. General Junot too is probably on his way to the spring."

Roland shrugged his shoulders. It was very evident that he thought the general's place was elsewhere, and that he had more important things demanding his attention than the beautiful daughters of Nazareth. Nevertheless, he followed the instructions given him, and soon reached the other end of the village.

The spring was about ten minutes' walk from the last house, and the road leading to it was bordered on each side by huge cactus-trees, which formed an impassable wall. Roland walked on, and soon espied the general and his two aids-de-camp standing a short distance from the spring, and watching the women who were passing to and fro.

Junot recognized the new-comer at once as Bonaparte's ordnance officer. The commander-in-chief's fondness for Roland was known to every one, and would in itself have been quite enough to make everybody smile upon him; but his courteous freedom of manner, and his wonderful courage, which was the talk of the army, would have gained him many friends even if he had been honored with a much smaller share of the general's favor.

Junot accordingly advanced to meet him, with hand cordially extended.

"Do you bring us good news, my dear Roland?" he asked.

"Yes, general, as I come to announce the near approach of the enemy," replied Roland.

"By my faith, next to the sight of these beautiful girls who carry their water-jugs like veritable princesses, I know of nothing that would afford me greater pleasure than the sight of the enemy," responded Junot. "Look, Roland! see what a queenly air the creatures have! Wouldn't you suppose they were so many goddesses? And when may we expect to see the enemy?"

"Quite as soon as you wish, I should say, general, as they are only five or six leagues from here."

"Do you know what these women answer when you tell them they are beautiful? 'It is the Virgin Mary's will.' This is the first time we have seen any pretty women since we came to Syria. Did you see them yourself, the enemy, I mean?"

"Yes; I saw them with my own eyes."

"Where are they coming from, and where are they going? What do they want with us?"

"They are coming from Damascus, and I presume they want to whip us. If I am not very much mistaken, they are going to Saint Jean d'Acre to raise the siege."

"Oh, in that case, we must cut them off. Are you going to stay with us or return to General Bonaparte?"

"I shall remain with you, general. I feel a strong desire to have a bout with the rascals. We are dying of *ennui* over there at Saint Jean d'Acre. Except for two or three sorties Djezzar has been stupid enough to make, there has been nothing to vary the monotony."

"Well, I think I can promise you some variety by to-morrow," responded Junot. "By the way, I forgot to ask how many there are of them."

"I will reply in the language of the Arab, general: 'As well try to count the sands of the sea.' There must be twenty-five or thirty thousand of them, I should say."

Junot scratched his head rather dubiously.

"The deuce!" he exclaimed; "then I can't do very much with the men I have here."

"How many men have you?" asked Roland.

"Exactly one hundred more than the three hundred Spartans. But we can do what they did, and that won't be so bad after all. However, it will be quite time enough to think of all that to-morrow. Would you like to see the curiosities of the town, or would you rather have some supper?"

"Well, here in Nazareth, interesting relics must be plentiful, general; but I won't try to conceal the fact that my stomach is much more clamorous than my eyes just now. I breakfasted off a few pieces of hard tack and a dozen dates this morning, on the banks of the Kishon, and I must admit that I am both hungry and thirsty."

"If you will do me the honor to sup with me we will do our best to appease your appetite. As for your thirst, you will never have a better opportunity to quench that."

And turning to a young girl who was passing, he said in Arabic:

"Water! Thy brother is thirsty."

And as he spoke he pointed to Roland.

She approached, tall and dignified, her tunic, with its long open sleeves, leaving her arms entirely bare. She lowered the jug she was carrying on her right shoulder until it was on a level with her left hand; then, with a graceful gesture, she offered the water to Roland, who drank long and deeply, not because the girl was beautiful, but because the water was fresh and cool.

"Has my brother had enough?" asked the girl.

"Yes; and thy brother thanks thee," replied Roland, in the same tongue.

The young girl bent her head with quiet dignity, replaced the jug on her shoulder, and walked on toward the village.

"Are you aware that you speak Arabic very fluently?" asked Junot, laughing.

"Wasn't I wounded and a prisoner among these rascals for a month at the time of the insurrection at Cairo?" said Roland. "I was obliged to learn a little Arabic in spite of myself, and since the commander-in-chief has found out that I can jabber a little in the prophet's tongue, he seems determined to take me about with him everywhere as an interpreter."

"Upon my soul! if I thought I could learn as much Arabic as you know in a month, I would be willing to pay the same price for the knowledge, and get myself wounded and taken prisoner to-morrow," responded Junot.

"Well, general," rejoined Roland, with the harsh, dry

laugh habitual with him, "if I might presume to offer my advice, it would be that you learn some other language and in a different manner. And now suppose we go to supper, general?"

And Roland walked on toward the village without deigning to bestow another glance on the beautiful Nazarenes whom Junot and his aids paused again and again to gaze at.

CHAPTER IX

THE BATTLE OF NAZARETH

At daybreak—that is to say, about six o'clock the next morning—the drums beat, and the trumpets sounded the *diane*.

As Roland had told Junot that the enemy's advance guard was on the way to Tiberias, Junot resolved not to give the Damascenes time to besiege him upon his mountain, crossed a ravine between the hills that surround Nazareth, and made his way down the valley as far as the village of Cana.

He did not see this village until he was but a quarter of a league from it, for a spur of the mountain almost conceals it from view.

The enemy might be either in the valley of Batouf or in the plain that lies at the foot of Mount Tabor; but be that as it might, as the French were coming down from the high places, as the Bible expresses it, they were in very little danger of being taken unawares, as they were almost sure to see the enemy from a distance.

The soldiers were more familiar with the miracle that Jesus performed at Cana than with any of the others, for it was at the wedding there that Jesus had turned the water into wine, and though the soldiers were very glad to get water in these days, it is certain that they would have been still happier if they could have got wine.

It was likewise at Cana that Jesus performed that other miracle described by Saint John:

"There was a certain nobleman, whose son was sick at Capernaum.

"When he heard that Jesus was come out of Judea into Galilee, he went unto him, and besought him that he would come down and heal his son, for he was at the point of death.

"Then Jesus said unto him, 'Except ye see signs and wonders ye will not believe.'

"The nobleman said unto him, 'Sir, come down ere my child die.'

"And Jesus said unto him, 'Go thy way; thy son liveth.' And the man believed the word that Jesus had spoken unto him and he went his way.

"And as he was now going down, his servants met him and told him, saying, 'Thy son liveth.'"

At the entrance to the village Junot found Sheik El Beled, who had come to beg him to proceed no further, as there were two or three thousand of the enemy's cavalry on the plain.

Junot had one hundred and fifty grenadiers of the Nineteenth Regiment of the line, one hundred and fifty carabineers, and one hundred cavalry, commanded by Major Duvivier, belonging to the Fourteenth Dragoons. This made exactly four hundred men, as he had said the night before. Junot thanked the sheik, but continued on his way, to the latter's great wonder and admiration. When he reached one of the branches of a small stream that takes its rise near Cana, he followed it until he came to the pass that separates Loubi from the mountains of Cana. Here he saw two or three thousand cavalry, divided into several different corps, galloping about between Mount Tabor and Loubi, and in order to obtain a better idea of their position, he galloped to a neighboring hill crowned with the ruins of a village known as Meschenah.

But just then he perceived another body of troops advancing upon the village of Loubi.

It was composed of Mamelukes, Turcomans, and Mangrabins. This body of troops was nearly, or quite as large as the other; so Junot, whose force consisted of only four hundred men, had at least five thousand to contend with.

Contrary to the custom of Orientals, these troops were advancing in a solid column, at a slow pace, and in excellent order. A large number of standards, banners, and horses' tails were visible in the ranks.

These horses' tails, which served as ensigns for the pashas, had afforded the French no little food for mirth until they heard the origin of this singular standard.

They learned that, at the battle of Nicopolis, Bajazet, having seen his standard captured by the Crusaders, had cut off his horse's tail with a blow of his saber, and placing it on a pike, had not only succeeded in rallying his followers around this strange standard, but had finally won this famous battle, one of the most disastrous to Christianity that ever took place.

Junot was right in believing that the body of troops which was now advancing in good order was the only one to be feared, and he only dispatched fifty grenadiers to keep back the cavalry he had seen first, for he felt sure that they were Bedouins who would confine themselves to harassing his troops during the fight.

But to oppose the other force he brought forward the other hundred grenadiers and his one hundred and fifty carabineers, reserving the one hundred dragoons in order to use them where they were most needed.

The Turks, seeing this handful of men stop and wait for them, supposed they were paralyzed with terror; so they approached within pistol range. But they had no sooner done this than each carabineer and grenadier, selecting his man, fired, and the entire front rank fell, while some of the bullets struck down the men and horses even as far back as in the third and fourth row.

This volley created great disorder among the Moslems, thus giving the grenadiers and carabineers time to reload; but this time only the front rank fired, after which the second rank passed forward their guns, receiving empty ones in their places. This continuous fire made the Turks waver; but when they noted their vastly superior numbers, they charged upon the enemy, shouting vociferously.

This was the moment Roland was waiting for. While Junot formed his two hundred and fifty men into a hollow square, Roland, placing himself at the head of the hundred dragoons, dashed forward and attacked the troops which were charging in a rather disorderly fashion on the flank.

The Turks were not used to the straight sabers, which pierced them like lances at a distance to which their curved blades could not reach, so the effect of the charge was murderous. The dragoons cut their way straight through the mass of Mussulmans; then they gave the troops formed in a square a chance to discharge their rifles, after which they dashed into the furrow the bullets had just plowed, enlarging the gap in such a fashion that the mass seemed to fall asunder, and the Turks, instead of continuing to advance with closed ranks, began to scatter over the plain.

Roland had attacked the standard-bearer of one of the principal chiefs, and having the curved saber of the chasseur instead of the straight-pointed blade of the dragoons, he and his opponent were on equal terms. Two or three times, letting the reins fall on his horse's neck, and guiding him by his legs, he placed his hands on his pistols; but he somehow felt that it would be unworthy of him to resort to this means of defense. So he urged his horse forward and seized his antagonist about the body, while the horses, apparently realizing that they, too, were enemies, bit and tore at each other. For a moment those who surrounded them paused in their strife—Frenchmen and Mussulmans alike—waiting to see the end; but suddenly Roland, loosening his girths, put spurs to his horse, which seemed to slip out from between his legs, while the weight of Roland's body dragged the Turk from his horse, and he fell face downward with one foot still in the stirrup. In a second Roland was on his feet again with a bloody saber in one hand and the Turkish standard in the other. As for the Mussulman, he was dead, and his horse, rendered frantic by a blow from Roland's saber, dragged him into the Moslem ranks, where he added to the disorder and confusion.

Meanwhile, the Arabs on the plains at the foot of Mount Tabor had hastened in the direction of the firing. Two chiefs, who were much better mounted than the others, preceded their men by about five hundred yards, and Junot rode out alone to meet them, bidding his soldiers leave them to him.

About one hundred yards from the fifty men, by whose aid he hoped to worst the Arabs from the plain, he paused, and seeing that he was now about twelve yards from the two horsemen, he allowed his saber to hang by its cord and snatched a pistol from his holster. Between the ears of one of the horses that were approaching he saw two blazing eyes, and being wonderfully skilful in the use of the pistol, as we have remarked before, he sent a bullet straight through the middle of their owner's forehead.

The rider fell; the horse, carried along by its own impetus, was caught by one of the grenadiers, and the general, replacing his pistol in the holster and seizing his saber, severed his other opponent's head from his body with a single blow.

After this, each officer—emulating his leader's example—quitted the ranks, and ten or a dozen single combats like that we have just described, ensued, in all of which the Turks were defeated.

The battle lasted from nine o'clock in the morning until three in the afternoon, when Junot ordered a gradual retreat into the mountains of Cana. He had realized that morning that while he might reasonably hope to make a brilliant fight with his four hundred men, he could not expect to come off completely victorious. The battle had been fought. Four hundred Frenchmen had held their ground for five hours against five thousand Turks; they had killed eight hundred of the enemy and wounded three hundred more. They themselves had had five men killed and one wounded.

Junot gave orders that this wounded man should be taken with them, and as his thigh was broken, they placed him on a litter, which four of his comrades carried in turn.

Roland had remounted his horse and exchanged his curved saber for a sword. He had in his holsters the pistols with which he could sever a pomegranate-flower from its stem at a distance of twenty yards. In company with Junot's two aids-de-camp he assumed command of the three hundred dragoons that composed the general's cavalry, and the three young men rivaled each other in their endeavors to make this work of death seem like a pleasure-party.

Whether fighting the Turks in hand-to-hand combats, or amusing themselves by using them as targets, their exploits furnished stirring anecdotes and amusing stories for the Army of the East for many a day.

At four o'clock Junot, established upon a plateau, with one of the tributaries of the little rivers that empty into the sea near Carmel at his feet, and in communication with the Greek and Catholic priests at Cana and Nazareth, was made safe from attack, and certain of his supplies by reason of his position, and could consequently wait composedly for the reenforcements which Napoleon, notified by the Sheik of Aher, was sure to send.

CHAPTER X

MOUNT TABOR

In accordance with Roland's expectations, the Sheik of Aher had reached the French camp at daybreak, and in accordance with Bonaparte's axiom, "Always wake me for bad news, but never for good news," the commander-in-chief had been awakened.

On being admitted into the general's presence, the sheik informed him that an army of about twenty-five thousand men had just crossed the Jordan, and when Bonaparte inquired what had become of Roland, the sheik replied that the young aid-de-camp had undertaken to warn Junot, who was at Nazareth.

Bonaparte had already sent some one to wake Bourrienne, and had also called for his map, and sent for Kléber.

In the presence of the last-named officer, the sheik made the young Druse point out the exact place at which the Moslems had crossed the river, the route they had taken afterward, and the road he and the sheik had taken on returning to camp.

"You will take your division, which must number about two thousand men," said Bonaparte to Kléber, "and proceed by the shortest route to Safarie. You ought to reach Nazareth by to-morrow morning. Have each of your men take sufficient water for the day, for though I see a river here on the map, I am very much afraid you will find it dried up at this season of the year. Let the battle take place on the plain near Loubi or Fouli, if possible. We must have our revenge for the battle of Tiberias, in which Saladin defeated Guy de Lusignan, in 1187. See that the Turks lose nothing by having waited all these years. Don't be uneasy about me; I shall get there in time."

Kléber got his division together and encamped that night near Safarie, a city which is said to have been honored by the presence of Saint Joachim and Saint Anne.

That same evening he opened communication with Junot, who had left an advance guard at Cana, and gone back to Nazareth, for which place he seemed to have a decided weakness. Kléber learned from him that the Mussulmans had not left Loubi; so they were to be found at one of the points indicated by Bonaparte, viz., the one in front, instead of behind, Mount Tabor.

A quarter of a league from Loubi was a village called Said Jarra, which was occupied by a portion of the Turkish army. The enemy's force at this point consisted of about seven or eight thousand men, and Kléber ordered Junot to make an attack upon it with a part of his division, while he himself charged upon the cavalry with the rest of his men formed in a square.

This plan was carried out, and in two hours the pasha's infantry was driven from Said Jarra and the cavalry from Loubi, after which the Turks, completely routed, beat a hasty retreat to the bank of the Jordan.

Junot had two horses killed under him in this engagement, and finding nothing in the way of a mount at hand except a dromedary, he mounted that and soon found himself in the midst of the Turks, among whom he loomed up like a giant.

But some one cut the ham-strings of his dromedary, and the animal fell, or, rather, sunk down beneath him. Fortunately, Roland had kept an eye on his comrade, and hastened to his assistance in company with Junot's aid-de-camp Teinturier.

Cutting their way through the crowd that surrounded Junot, they soon reached his side and mounted him on the horse of a dead Mameluke, after which all three, pistols in hand, forced their way through the living wall, and reappeared in the midst of the French soldiers, who had believed them dead, and were pressing forward resolved to recover their bodies.

Kléber had moved so rapidly that his army wagons had not been able to keep up with him, so for want of ammunition he was now unable to pursue the fugitives; so he fell back upon Nazareth and fortified his position at Safarie.

On the 13th, Kléber sent out scouts to reconnoiter, and they found that the Mamelukes of Ibrahim Bey, the janissaries of Damascus, and the Arabs of Aleppo, as well as many belonging to the various Syrian tribes, had united with the people of Nabloos, and were now encamped on the plain of Esdrelon, near Fouli.

Kléber immediately notified the commander-in-chief of these facts. He also told him that the hostile army consisted of about thirty thousand men, about twenty-five thousand of whom were mounted, but that he intended to make an attack upon this multitude the next day with his twenty-five hundred men. He concluded his letter with these words:

"The enemy is exactly where you want him. Try to join us at the *fête.*"

This dispatch was intrusted to the Sheik of Aher; but as the plain was covered with hostile riders, three copies were sent by as many different messengers and by as many different routes.

Bonaparte received two of these three dispatches—one at eleven o'clock at night, the other at one o'clock in the morning. The third messenger was never heard from.

Bonaparte had no intention of not being present at the *fête*. He was extremely anxious to bring about a general engagement, or, rather, a decisive battle that would drive back this formidable host which threatened to crush him against the walls of Saint Jean d'Acre.

So, at two o'clock in the morning, Murat was sent on ahead with one thousand infantry, one field-piece, and a detachment of dragoons. He had orders to advance as far as the river Jordan, and there take possession of Jacob's Bridge, in order to cut off the retreat of the Turkish army. He had about ten leagues to travel.

Bonaparte started at three in the afternoon, taking with him every man that was not absolutely required to keep the enemy within their walls. At daybreak he halted on the heights of Safarie and distributed bread, water, and brandy among his men. He had been obliged to take the longest route, as his artillery and wagons could not follow him along the banks of the Kishon. At nine o'clock he started again, and at ten in the morning he had reached the foot of Mount Tabor. There, about ten leagues away, he saw Kléber's division, barely twenty-five hundred strong, drawn up face to face with the Moslem army, which surrounded it on all sides and made it look like a black spot encircled with fire.

More than twenty thousand cavalry were attacking it, now revolving around it like a whirlwind, now rushing down upon it like an avalanche. Never before had these men, who had witnessed so many wonders, seen such an immense number of horsemen in motion, and yet each soldier maintained his coolness, firing only when he was sure of his man, striking at the horses with his bayonet when they came too near, but reserving his bullets for their riders.

Each soldier had received fifty cartridges that morning, but at eleven o'clock it became necessary to distribute fifty more, and having fired one hundred thousand bullets with deadly aim, they had piled up a high breastwork of dead horses and men around them, which protected them as effectually as any rampart could have done.

This was the sight that greeted the eyes of Bonaparte and his army when they rounded Mount Tabor, and enthusiastic shouts of, "To the enemy! to the enemy!" burst from every lip.

But Bonaparte made them take a quarter of an hour for rest, for he knew that Kléber could hold out for hours if necessary, and he wanted the day's work to be thoroughly done.

Then he formed his six thousand troops into two squares of three thousand men each, and placed them in such a manner as to inclose the whole savage horde, both cavalry and infantry, in a triangle of fire and steel.

The combatants were so deeply in earnest that, like the Romans and Carthaginians, who, during the battle of Thrasymine, were not even conscious of the earthquake that overthrew twenty-two cities—neither the Turks nor the French were aware of the approach of Bonaparte's army, whose weapons emitted dazzling gleams of lightning, precursors of the storm that was about to burst forth.

Suddenly a single cannon-shot was heard. It was the signal by which Bonaparte had agreed to announce his approach. The three squares were now not more than half a league from each other, and their triple fire was about to be directed upon a compact mass of twenty-five thousand men.

The fire burst forth from all three sides simultaneously. The Mamelukes and janissaries—in short, all the cavalry—turned first this way, then that, not knowing how to make their escape from this fiery furnace, while the ten thousand infantry, ignorant of all military science and tactics, broke ranks, and hurled themselves madly upon the three lines of fire; but in less than an hour the fugitives had disappeared like dust swept on by the wind, leaving the plain covered with dead, and abandoning their camp, standards, four hundred camels, and an immense amount of ammunition and provisions.

The fugitives who escaped this deadly fire fancied they were safe, and those who were fortunate enough to reach the mountains of Nabloos did find a refuge there; but those who attempted to cross the Jordan found Murat and his one thousand men guarding the ford.

The French did not stop until they became weary of slaughter.

Bonaparte and Kléber met upon the battle-field and embraced each other amid the enthusiastic shouts of the soldiers.

It was then, tradition says, that the gigantic Kléber, placing his hand on the shoulder of Bonaparte, whose head barely reached his subordinate's breast, uttered those words which have created so much controversy since:

"General, you are as great as the world!"

Bonaparte might well have been content, for it was upon the very spot where Guy de Lusignan had been defeated that he had just conquered.

It was upon this very spot that the French, on the 5th of July, 1187, "having exhausted even the sources of their tears," says one Arab writer, met the Mussulmans, commanded by Saladin, in mortal combat.

"At first they fought like lions," this same writer goes on to say, "but toward the last they were no more dangerous than frightened sheep." Hemmed in on all sides, they were driven back to the foot of that Mountain of the Beatitudes, where our Saviour once said:

"Blessed are the poor in spirit, blessed are they who weep, blessed are they who are persecuted for righteousness' sake," and where he also said, "When ye pray after this manner pray ye: Our Father who art in heaven."

The whole engagement took place in the immediate neighborhood of this mountain which the infidels call Mount Hittin.

Guy de Lusignan took refuge upon it, and defended the True Cross to the very best of his ability; but he could not prevent the Mussulmans from securing possession of it after they had mortally wounded the Bishop of Saint Jean d'Acre, who was bearing it.

Raymond cut his way out with his men, and made his escape to Tripoli, where he died of grief.

As long as a single group of horsemen remained they returned valiantly to the charge, but only to melt away before the Saracens like wax in a furnace.

Finally the king's pavilion fell, to rise no more.

Guy de Lusignan was taken prisoner, and Saladin, taking the sword of the King of Jerusalem from the person who brought it to him, dismounted from his horse and returned devout thanks to Mohammed for his victory.

Never before in Palestine or anywhere else had any Christian army ever suffered such defeat. "On looking at the dead," says an eye-witness, "one could not believe there were any prisoners; on looking at the prisoners, one could not believe there were any dead."

The king, after promising to renounce his authority, was sent to Damascus. All the Knights of the Temple and Hospitallers lost their heads.

Saladin, who feared his soldiers might feel more compassion than he did, and spare some of these soldier monks, offered to pay thirty pieces of gold for each prisoner that was brought to him.

Out of the entire Christian army barely one thousand men escaped. Arabian historians say a prisoner was sold for a pair of sandals, and that the heads of Christians were piled up like melons in the streets of Damascus.

Monseigneur Mislin, in his valuable book, entitled "Holy Places," says that on crossing the plain of Hittin a year after this terrible battle, he still saw heaps of bones, and that the neighboring mountains and valleys were covered with bodies the wild beasts had dragged there.

Surely, after the battle of Mount Tabor, the jackals of the plain of Esdrelon had no cause to envy the hyenas of Mount Tiberias.

CHAPTER XI

A CLEVER EXPEDIENT

Since Bonaparte's return from Mount Tabor, nearly a month before, the batteries had not ceased to thunder for a single day, nor had there been even a momentary truce between besiegers and besieged.

This was the first case of prolonged opposition chance had placed in Bonaparte's path.

The siege of Saint Jean d'Acre lasted sixty days. There were seven assaults and twelve sorties. Caffarelli had died from the amputation of his arm, and Croisier was still languishing on a bed of suffering.

More than a thousand men had been killed or had died of the plague.

There was plenty of powder still, but no bullets, and this fact soon became known to the army. Matters like this cannot be concealed from soldiers.

One morning, while Bonaparte and Roland were both in the trench, a sergeant-major approached the latter, and asked:

"Is it true that we are in need of shot, commandant?"

"Yes. Why do you ask?" responded Roland.

"Because, if the commander-in-chief wants some I know a way to get them for him," replied the sergeant-major, with that twitch of the neck that was habitual with him and that seemed to date back to the time he first wore a cravat.

"You?"

"Yes, I. And they won't cost him so much, either—only five sous apiece."

"Five sous! Why, they cost the government forty."

"Yes; so you see you would be making an excellent bargain."

"You're not joking?"

"Do you suppose I would presume to joke with my superior officer?"

Roland went to Bonaparte and repeated what the sergeant major had just said.

"These rascals have very clever ideas sometimes," said the commander-in-chief. "Call him."

So Roland motioned the sergeant to approach.

He advanced with a military stride, then paused about six feet from Bonaparte, with his hand touching the visor of his helmet.

"Are you the dealer in bullets?" asked Bonaparte.

"I sell them; I do not manufacture them."

"And you will contract to furnish them for five sous?"

"Yes, general."

"But how will you do it?"

"That is my secret. If I were to tell it, everybody would be selling them."

"And how many can you furnish?"

"As many as you want."

"And what do you need in order to obtain them?" asked Bonaparte.

"Permission to go in bathing with my company."

Bonaparte burst into a hearty laugh. He understood the scheme now.

"Very well, go," he replied.

The sergeant-major saluted and then started off on a run.

In a few moments the commander-in-chief and his aid saw pass, with the sergeant-major at its head, the company that had received permission to bathe.

"Come and see something curious," Bonaparte remarked to his aid-de-camp; and taking Roland's arm, he ascended a small knoll which commanded a view of the entire gulf.

Here he saw the sergeant-major remove his clothing and wade into the sea with a part of his company, while the others scattered themselves along the beach.

Until then Roland had not understood the scheme, but the sergeant-major and his comrades were no sooner in the water than a thick shower of bullets began to fall upon them from the ramparts as well as from the two English frigates; but as the soldiers who were in the water, as well as those who were on the beach, took good care to keep quite a distance from each other, the bullets fell in the spaces between the men, where they were immediately picked up without a single one being lost, not even one of those that fell into the water, for as the beach sloped very gradually, the soldiers were only obliged to stoop to pick up the bullets from the bottom.

This curious game lasted two hours.

True, at the end of that time three men had been killed, but the inventor of the scheme had collected from ten to twelve hundred bullets, which netted the company three hundred francs.

One hundred francs for each man killed! The company thought that an excellent bargain.

As the guns on the frigates and in the city were all of the same caliber as those of our army—that is to say, twelve and sixteen—every bullet could be used.

On the following day the company went in bathing again. When he heard the firing, Bonaparte could not resist the temptation to witness the curious spectacle again, and this time several of the army officers accompanied him.

Roland could hardly contain himself. He was one of those men who seem to be positively intoxicated by the smell of powder.

With two bounds he was on the beach, and tossing his clothing on the sand, and retaining only his drawers, he threw himself into the sea.

"What is the matter with that foolish fellow that he seems to be always trying to find a way to get killed?" muttered Bonaparte.

But Roland was no longer there to reply, and it is more than likely that he would not have replied if he had been.

Bonaparte watched him as he swam out past the bathers and almost within musket range of the "Tiger." They opened fire upon him, and the bullets made the water leap and dance around him.

He did not trouble himself in the least about them, however, and his conduct seemed such a direct challenge that an officer aboard the "Tiger" ordered a boat lowered.

Roland did not object to being killed, but he did decidedly object to being taken prisoner; so he swam out vigorously toward the reefs that lie along the base of the fortress, knowing that it was impossible for a boat to follow him there.

For a minute or two he vanished from sight entirely, and Bonaparte was really beginning to fear that he had been killed, when he saw him suddenly reappear close to the foot of the city walls under a brisk fire of musketry. But Roland seemed to have entered into a compact with the bullets, for he walked slowly back along the beach, though the sand on one side and the water on the other were thrown up almost under his very feet, and soon reaching the place where he had dropped his clothes, he dressed himself and then walked toward Bonaparte.

A vivandière who had joined the party, and who was distributing the contents of her cask among the collectors of bullets, offered him a glass.

"Ah, so it is you, Goddess of Reason!" said Roland. "You know very well that I never drink brandy."

"No; but once in a life-time doesn't matter, you know,

and you certainly deserve a drop or two after what you have done."

And as she spoke, she held out a tiny silver cup filled with liquor.

"Drink to the health of the commander-in-chief and to the capture of Saint Jean d'Acre," she exclaimed.

Roland drank, raising his glass and bowing to Bonaparte, after which he offered the vivandière a piece of silver.

"Nonsense!" she exclaimed. "I sell my liquor to those who need to buy courage, not to you. Besides, my husband is likely to make a very good thing out of this."

"What is your husband doing?"

"He is the bullet merchant."

"Ah! Well, by the sound of the cannonading, I should think he was likely to make his fortune in a very short time. Where is this husband of yours?"

"Over there," she replied, pointing out to Roland the same sergeant-major who had offered to furnish bullets for five sous apiece.

As the Goddess of Reason spoke, a shell buried itself in the sand not more than four feet from the daring speculator, who instantly threw himself face downward on the ground and remained perfectly motionless.

About three seconds afterward the shell burst, scattering a cloud of sand around.

"Upon my word, Goddess of Reason, I'm very much afraid that shot made you a widow!" exclaimed Roland.

But the sergeant-major emerged from the blinding cloud of dust and sand unhurt, though it looked very much as if he were rising out of the mouth of a volcano.

"Long live the Republic!" he shouted as he shook himself.

And this cry, instantly taken up by actors and spectators alike, echoed and re-echoed over the water and beach, and seemed to make the very dead immortal.

CHAPTER XII

HOW CITIZEN PIERRE CLAUDE FARAUD WAS MADE A SUB-LIEUTENANT

This garnering of shot continued four days; but finally the English and Turks seemed to suspect the object of the game which they had at first mistaken for mere bravado.

When the bullets were counted, they found that three thousand four hundred had been picked up, and Bonaparte paid for every one of them through Estève, the paymaster of the army.

"Ah! so you are speculating again?" exclaimed Estève, recognizing an old acquaintance in the sergeant. "I had to pay you for a cannon at Froeschwillers, and now I have to pay you for thirty-four hundred shot at Saint Jean d'Acre."

"I am none the richer for it, though," responded the sergeant. "The six hundred francs made at Froeschwillers, together with much of the Prince de Condé's treasure, went for pensions to the widows and orphans made at Dawendorff."

"And what are you going to do with this money?"

"I have a use for it."

"May I ask what it is?"

"Certainly, as I shall have to ask you to undertake the commission. This money is intended for the aged mother of our brave Captain Guillet, who was slain during the last assault. He bequeathed her to the care of his company before he died. The Republic is not very rich, and might forget to pay her a pension, so we think it will be well for her to have a little money of her own. It's a pity, though, that those devilish Englishmen and Turks should have found out our little game and refused to help us out in it any longer."

"Where does Captain Guillet's mother live?"

"At Chateauroux."

"Very well, the amount shall be paid over to her in the name of the Third Company of the Thirty-second Brigade, and of—"

"Of Pierre Claude Faraud, executor."

"Thanks. And now, Pierre Claude Faraud, the commander-in-chief wishes me to say that he desires to speak with you soon."

"Whenever he pleases—Pierre Claude Faraud is never averse to a friendly chat with anybody."

Bonaparte was at dinner in his tent when he was told that the sergeant he had sent for was awaiting his pleasure.

"Show him in," said Bonaparte. "Ah! so it's you;" he added, as Faraud entered.

"Yes, Citizen General; didst *thou* not send for me?" responded Faraud.

"To what brigade do you belong?"

"The Thirty-second."

"And to what company?"

"The Third."

"What captain?"

"Captain Guillet, deceased."

"And has no one been appointed to his place?"

"No one."

"Which of the two lieutenants is the braver?"

"There is no one person braver than another in the Thirty-second. All are equally brave."

"Which is the elder, then?"

"Lieutenant Valato, who remained at his post after being shot through the breast."

"Then the second lieutenant was not wounded?"

"No; but that was not his fault."

"Very well; Valato shall be captain, and the second lieutenant will take the rank of first lieutenant. Now, is there no under officer who has distinguished himself?"

"All our men distinguished themselves."

"But I cannot make them all lieutenants, you idiot!"

"That's a fact. Well, there is Taberly—"

"Who is Taberly?"

"A very brave man."

"And would his promotion be well received?"

"Everybody would be delighted."

"Well, there will still be a vacant lieutenancy. Who is the eldest orderly-sergeant?"

The man he was questioning made a sudden movement of the neck as if his cravat were strangling him.

"Pierre Claude Faraud," he replied.

"What have you got to say about him?"

"Not much of anything."

"Possibly you do not know him."

"On the contrary, it is because I do know him."

"Well, I knew him too."

"You do, general?"

"Yes. He is an Aristocrat of the Army of the Rhine—a quarrelsome fellow whom I caught fighting a duel with a Republican at Milan, and whom I sent to the guard-house for forty-eight hours."

"Twenty-four, general."

"Then I cheated him out of his other twenty-four."

"He is ready to take them, general, at any time."

"But a sub-lieutenant is not put in the guard-house; he is only placed under arrest."

"But Pierre Claude Faraud is not a sub-lieutenant, general; he is only an orderly-sergeant?"

"Yes, he is a sub-lieutenant."

"Since when, pray?"

"Since this morning. You see what it is to have influential friends."

"I have influential friends?" exclaimed Faraud.

"Oh, ho! so you are the man?"

"Yes, general; and I should like to know who my influential friends are."

"I," replied Estève, "who have twice seen you generously give away money you had richly earned."

"And I," said Roland, "who want a brave man to assist me in an expedition from which few are likely to return."

"Take him," said Bonaparte; "but don't place him on guard, and don't take him to any place where there are any wolves."

"What! you have heard that story, general?"

"I have heard everything, monsieur."

"Ah! Citizen General, thou art the man who ought to take my twenty-four hours in the guardhouse."

"Why?"

"Didst thou not say 'monsieur' just now?"

"Come, come! you are a sharp fellow," exclaimed Bonaparte, laughing. "I shall remember you. In the meantime, you must drink to the health of the Republic."

"Citizen Faraud never drinks to the health of the Republic in anything but brandy," said Roland, laughing.

"The deuce! and I have none."

"I have provided for such an emergency," said Roland; and stepping to the door of the tent, he called: "Come in, citizeness."

It was the Goddess of Reason who appeared in answer to the summons.

She was still very handsome, though the bright sunlight of Egypt had made her complexion much darker.

"Rose here?" exclaimed Faraud, in evident surprise.

"So you know this citizeness?" asked Roland, laughing.

"I should think so. She is my wife."

"Citizeness, I saw you at your work in the midst of a

heavy fire of shot and shell," said Bonaparte. "Roland wanted to pay you for the brandy you gave him when he came out of the water, but you refused to take his money. As I had no brandy, and each of my guests wished a glass, Roland suggested that we call the Goddess of Reason and settle the entire score at once, so we sent for you."

The Goddess of Reason poured from the little cask a glass for all except Faraud. She seemed to overlook him.

"Everybody drinks when it is the health of the Republic that is proposed," remarked Roland.

"But any one is at liberty to drink the toast in water if he chooses," said Bonaparte.

And raising his glass:

"To the health of the Republic!" he cried.

And the toast was repeated in chorus, after which Roland, drawing an official-looking document from his pocket, said:

"Here is a bill of exchange on posterity, only it is drawn in your husband's name. You can indorse it, but he alone can draw it."

The Goddess of Reason, with trembling hand, unfolded the parchment at which Faraud was gazing with sparkling eyes.

"See, Pierre!" she cried, holding it out to him. "It is your commission as sub-lieutenant in Taberly's place!"

"Is that true?" asked Faraud.

"See for yourself."

Faraud looked.

"Hurah, Sub-lieutenant Faraud!" he exclaimed. "Long live General Bonaparte!"

"Consider yourself under arrest for twenty-four hours for having cried 'Long live General Bonaparte!' instead of 'Long live the Republic!'" said Bonaparte.

"There is no such thing as getting out of it, it seems," replied Faraud; "but I'll do those twenty-four hours with pleasure."

CHAPTER XIII

THE FINAL ASSAULT

During the night that followed Faraud's promotion, Bonaparte received eight pieces of heavy artillery and an abundant supply of ammunition.

The shot Faraud had secured had served to repulse the sorties from the beleaguered town, and the Accursed Tower having been almost entirely destroyed, Bonaparte resolved to make one more assault.

Circumstances, too, made it imperative that he should do so, for on the 8th of May a Turkish fleet of thirty vessels, attended by several English war-ships, was sighted.

It was scarcely daybreak when Bonaparte was informed of the fact, and he at once decided that this fleet was coming from the Isle of Rhodes laden with re-enforcements, provisions, and ammunition for the besieged; so Saint Jean d'Acre must be taken, if possible, before the number of the garrison was doubled.

When Roland learned that an immediate attack had been decided upon, he asked the commander-in-chief for two hundred men, with *carte blanche* to do whatever he pleased with them.

But Napoleon insisted upon an explanation, for though he knew Roland's courage, the fact that this courage amounted to positive rashness, made him hesitate to intrust the lives of two hundred men to him.

So Roland explained that on the day he took his long bath in the sea he had discerned from the water a breach in the fortifications which could not be seen from the land, and concerning which the garrison apparently felt no uneasiness, defended as it was by an inside battery and by the fire from the English vessels.

Through this breach he intended to enter the town and create a diversion with his two hundred men, and Bonaparte finally gave him the desired permission.

Roland selected his two hundred men from the Thirty-second Brigade, and the new sub-lieutenant Faraud was one of the number.

Bonaparte ordered a general attack. Murat, Rampon, Vial, Kléber, and Junot, generals of division, generals of brigade, and corps commanders were all to charge at once.

By ten o'clock in the morning all the outer works which had been retaken by the enemy had been again demolished, five flags taken, three cannon captured and four spiked; but the garrison did not yield an inch of ground. As fast as the first defenders were killed, others took their places. Never since the time that religious enthusiasm placed the sword in the hands of the Crusaders, and Mohammedan fanaticism the cimeter in the hands of the Turks, had such a violent and sanguinary struggle, struck terror to the hearts of a populace, one-third of whom prayed for the success of the Christians, and the remaining two-thirds for the success of the Djezzar. From the ramparts, upon which they had gained a partial foothold, and from which shouts of victory were already resounding, the French soldiers could see the Moslem women rushing wildly through the streets, throwing dust on their heads and uttering shrill cries, which resembled at once the hooting of owls and the yelling of hyenas—cries which no person that heard them could ever forget.

Generals, officers, and privates, all fought together in the trenches. Kléber, armed with an Albanian rifle—which he had wrested from its owner—used it as a club, and raising it high above his head, as a thresher raises a flail, felled a man at every blow.

Murat, with head bare and long hair floating in the wind, was swinging his saber swiftly to and fro, slaying every man that came in contact with his blade; while Junot, now with a rifle, now with a pistol, killed an opponent every time he fired.

Boyer, the commander of the Eighteenth Brigade, fell in the *mêlée* with seventeen officers and more than one hundred and fifty of his men; but Lannes, Bon, and Vial rushed on over their bodies, which served to bring them a little nearer on a level with the ramparts.

Bonaparte, not standing in the trench, but upon the edge of it, directing the artillery himself, a target for every shot, was endeavoring to make a breach in the wall on his right with the cannon captured in the tower.

At the end of an hour there seemed to be a practicable opening.

They had no brush with which to fill up the ditch, so they threw in dead bodies as they had done elsewhere. Mussulmans, Christians, Frenchmen, and Turks hurled from the windows of the tower where they lay in heaps; formed a bridge as high as the ramparts.

Shouts of "Long live the Republic!" mingled with cries of "On, on!" were heard.

The bands played the "Marseillaise," and all the rest of the army took part in the fight.

Bonaparte sent one of his aids to tell Roland that the time for him to divert the enemy's attention had come; but when he learned what was to be attempted, Raimbaud asked Roland to allow him to remain with him instead of returning to Bonaparte.

The two young men were great friends, and when a battle is going on one does not refuse a friend favors of that sort.

Faraud had succeeded in securing possession of the coat

and epaulettes of a dead sub-lieutenant, and now shone resplendent at the head of his company.

The Goddess of Reason, even more elated by his promotion than he was, marched beside him, with a pair of pistols in her belt.

As soon as Roland received the order he placed himself at the head of his two hundred men, plunged into the water with them, rounded the bastion, with the water reaching above their waists, and suddenly presented himself at the breach, the trumpets blaring loudly all the while.

The attack was so unexpected that the gunners were not even ready with their pieces; so Roland took possession of the guns, and having no men to handle them, spiked them.

Then, with deafening shout of "Victory! victory !" they dashed into the winding streets of the town.

These shouts were heard upon the ramparts, and greatly increased the energy and ardor of the besiegers.

For a second time Bonaparte believed himself master of Saint Jean d'Acre, and rushed into the Accursed Tower which they had had so much difficulty in capturing.

But when he entered it he saw, with dismay, a second inclosure by which our soldiers had been brought to a standstill. It was one that Colonel Phélippeaux, Bonaparte's schoolmate at Brienne, had ordered constructed behind the first.

Leaning half-way out of the window, Bonaparte did his best to encourage his soldiers. The grenadiers, furious at finding themselves confronted by still another obstacle, tried to climb upon one another's shoulders for want of ladders; but all at once, while the besiegers were attacked in front by those who had been stationed there to defend the inclosure, their flank was swept by a heavy cross-fire, and a violent fusillade burst forth from the houses, streets, barricades, and even from Djezzar's seraglio. A dense smoke, too, was rising from the interior of the town. It was caused by Roland, Raimbaud, and Faraud, who had set fire to a bazaar. Suddenly they appeared on the roofs of the houses, evidently in the hope of establishing communication with those on the ramparts.

Through the smoke of the fire and that made by the artillery, the French on the ramparts saw tricolored plumes waving, and a cry of "Victory!" went up for the third time that day, but it was destined to be the last.

The soldiers, who had been expected to effect a junction with Roland's men by way of the rampart and a number of whom had already jumped down into the town while their comrades were still fighting on the ramparts or in the trenches, being assailed by a quadruple fusillade, wavered as the bullets and cannon-balls whistled and roared around them.

Lannes, wounded in the head by a bullet, sunk upon his knees, but was picked up and carried away by his grenadiers; Kléber was still holding his own in the midst of the terrific fire, like the invulnerable giant that he was. Bon and Vial were both driven back into the trenches.

Bonaparte looked around in vain for some one to support Kléber, but everybody's attention seemed to be fully occupied; so, with tears of rage in his eyes, he gave orders to sound the retreat, for he did not doubt that all who had entered the town with Roland, as well as those who had slipped down off the rampart—two hundred and fifty or three hundred in all—were lost.

He was the last to retire from the trench, and subsequently shut himself up in his tent after giving strict orders that he was on no account to be disturbed.

This was the first time in three years that he had ever doubted his ultimate success.

What a sublime page might be written by the historian who could describe the thoughts that passed through his mind in this hour of despair!

CHAPTER XIV

THE LAST BULLETIN

Meanwhile, Roland's party, together with the fifty men who had dropped down into the city and joined him after having believed for a time that they were sure to be supported, began to think that they had been abandoned, for the shouts of victory which had answered theirs became fainter and fainter until they finally died away altogether. The volleys of musketry and artillery, too, rang out at longer and longer intervals until at the end of an hour they ceased entirely, and several times Roland even thought he heard the drums and bugles sounding the retreat.

Then all sounds suddenly ceased, and there came rushing in upon the little band from all sides simultaneously, like a mighty tide, English, Turks, Mamelukes, Arnauts, and Albanians—in short, the entire garrison of nearly eight thousand men.

Roland formed his little company into a square, with one side resting upon a mosque. In this mosque he placed fifty of his men, thus converting it into a sort of fortress; then, after he had made them take a solemn oath to defend themselves to the death against enemies they knew would grant them no quarter, they awaited with fixed bayonets the coming of the foe.

The Turks, confident of the success of their cavalry, as usual, hurled it upon the little band with such fury that though the double volley fired by the French laid at least sixty men and horses low, those behind them dashed over their prostrate bodies and flung themselves upon the still smoking bayonets.

But there they were obliged to pause.

The second row of French soldiers had had time to reload, and now fired.

The Turks had no alternative but to retreat; but as they could not repass the mountain of wounded and dead, they tried to escape to the right or to the left, but two terrific volleys accompanied them in their flight, mowing them down in swathes.

But in a moment they returned again, even more determined and desperate.

Then a terrible struggle began—a hand-to-hand fight, in which the Turkish horsemen rushed up to the very points of our bayonets to discharge their pistols.

Others, seeing that the reflection of the sun on the barrels of the guns frightened their horses, made them walk backward, then compelling them to rear, threw themselves over with the animals upon the bayonets, while the wounded dragged themselves along on the ground, and gliding under the gun-barrels like serpents, ham-strung our soldiers.

Roland, armed with a double-barreled gun—his favorite weapon for this kind of fighting—laid a chief low each time he fired.

Faraud, who was in the mosque, directed the operations there, and more than one arm that held an uplifted saber dropped helpless and inert, hit by a bullet from some window in the gallery of the minaret.

Roland, seeing that his force was diminishing greatly in numbers, and that, in spite of the wall of corpses, which formed a rampart around his little band, he could not maintain such an unequal struggle for any great length of time, ordered the door of the mosque opened, and with great coolness, and continuing his murderous fire all the while, made his men enter, being himself the last to pass through the door.

The firing was then resumed through every available opening in the mosque; but the Turks brought up a piece of artillery, and brought it to bear upon the door.

Roland was standing at one of the windows, and shot down, one after another in quick succession, three gunners who approached the gun to apply a match to the touch-hole. At last a horseman rode swiftly past the gun, and before any one could divine his intention, fired his pistol at the priming.

The gun went off, and horse and rider rolled over and over for a distance of ten yards, but the door was shattered. Yet, through this broken door there came such a terrible fusillade that, though the Turks came up three times to enter the mosque, they were repulsed each time.

Frantic with rage, they rallied and made another attempt; but this time only a few desultory shots responded to their vengeful shouts.

The ammunition was exhausted; but undaunted, our grenadiers awaited the enemy with fixed bayonets.

"Friends!" said Roland, "remember that you have sworn to die rather than be taken prisoners by Djezzar the Butcher, who cut off our comrades' heads!"

"We swear it!" cried Roland's men, as if with a single voice.

"Long live the Republic!" shouted Roland.

"Long live the Republic!" they all repeated after him in chorus.

And while each man prepared to die, he resolved to sell his life as dearly as possible.

Just then a party of English officers, with Sidney Smith at their head, appeared at the door. They all carried their swords in their scabbards.

Smith raised his hat and indicated with a gesture that he wished to speak. There was a profound silence.

"Gentlemen," he said in excellent French, "you are brave men, and it shall never be said that men who have conducted themselves like heroes were massacred in my presence. Surrender, and I pledge you my word that your lives shall be spared."

"That is saying too much or not enough," replied Roland, promptly.

"What more do you want, pray?"

"Kill us to the very last man, or let us all go free."

"You are rather exacting, gentlemen; but one can refuse men like you nothing," responded the commodore. "But you will permit me, will you not, to furnish you with an escort of English soldiers as far as the gate of the city? Otherwise, I assure you, that not one of you will reach it alive. Is that agreed?"

"Yes, my lord," replied Roland; "and we can only thank you deeply for your courtesy."

Ten minutes afterward the English escort arrived, and the French soldiers with fixed bayonets, and the officers with drawn swords, passed through the streets leading to the French camp amid the muttered curses of the men, the shrill vituperation of the women, and the derisive yells of the children.

Ten or twelve wounded men, one of whom was Faraud, were carried on hastily improvised litters constructed of gun-barrels.

The Goddess of Reason walked beside her husband's litter, pistol in hand.

Smith and his English soldiers did not leave the grenadiers until they were beyond the reach of the Turkish guns, and the red-coats presented arms as the grenadiers filed by.

Bonaparte had retired to the seclusion of his own tent, as we have remarked before. Calling for Plutarch, he reread the life Augustus, and thinking of Roland and his gallant comrades who were doubtless being ruthlessly slaughtered, he murmured, like Augustus, after the battle of Teutberg: "Varus, give me back my legions!"

There was no one of whom he could demand his legions, however, for he was his own Varus.

Suddenly he heard a great commotion in the camp, and the strains of the "Marseillaise" reached his ears.

Why were they rejoicing and singing, these soldiers, while their leader was weeping with grief and rage?

He sprung to the door of his tent, and there stood Roland, his aid-de-camp, Raimbaud, and Sub-lieutenant Faraud, perched upon one leg like a heron, his other leg having been broken by a bullet.

The wounded man was resting one hand on the shoulder of the Goddess of Reason.

Behind them were the two hundred men Bonaparte had been mourning as lost.

"Ah! my friend," the commander-in-chief joyfully exclaimed, pressing Roland's hand, "I feared it was all over with you. How did you manage to get out of the scrape?"

"Raimbaud will explain," answered Roland, out of humor because he owed his life to an Englishman. "I am too thirsty to talk; I must have something to drink."

And picking up a glass of water that was standing on the table, he drained it at a single draught, while Bonaparte stepped out to greet the little body of soldiers, all the more delighted to see them as he had abandoned all hope of ever beholding them again.

CHAPTER XV

VANISHED HOPES

Napoleon, in speaking of Saint Jean d'Acre one day at Saint Helena, said:

"The fate of the Orient depended upon that insignificant town. If Saint Jean d'Acre had been taken, I would have changed the whole face of the world."

This regret, so forcibly expressed twenty years afterward, gives one some conception of what Bonaparte must have suffered when forced to admit the impossibility of taking Saint Jean d'Acre. He published the following general order in all the divisions of the army.

As usual, Bourrienne wrote it at his dictation, and it read as follows:

"SOLDIERS,—You have crossed the desert that divides Africa from Asia more swiftly than any army of Arabs could have done.

"The army that was on its way to invade Egypt is no more. You have captured its commander, its camp equipments, its baggage, its supplies, and its camels.

"You have taken all the desert strongholds. On the plains of Mount Tabor you have scattered that immense army gathered from all parts of Asia, in the hope of pillaging Egypt.

"At last, after having, with a mere handful of men, maintained a war for three months in the heart of Syria, captured forty pieces of artillery, fifty flags, and six thousand prisoners, and demolished the fortifications of Gaza, Jaffa, and Kaiffa, we are about to return to Egypt.

"A few days more and you might reasonably hope to capture the pasha in his own palace; but at this season of the year the Castle of Acre will not compensate for the loss of even a few days, and the brave men I should lose are needed for other and more important operations.

"Soldiers, we have a season of danger and fatigue before us. Having made it impossible for the East to do us any further serious injury in this campaign, we may now be obliged to resist the encroachments of a part of the west.

"You will find new opportunities to win glory, and if in a time of so many battles each day is necessarily marked by the loss of some brave men, other brave men must take their places in the little band who set such a brilliant example of daring, and who make victory so easy for their leader."

As he concluded the dictation of this bulletin, Bonaparte rose and went out of the tent as if to breathe more freely.

Bourrienne followed him anxiously.

Events seldom made such a deep impression on that heart of bronze.

Bonaparte climbed the little hill that overlooked the camp, and seating himself on a stone, remained for a long time with his eyes fixed upon the partially demolished fortress and the watery waste which stretched before him in all its immensity.

Finally he said as if to himself:

"The men who will write the history of my life will not understand why I fought so long and desperately for this miserable little place. Ah! if I could only have taken it, as I hoped to do!"

He let his head drop upon his hands.

"And if you had taken it?" asked Bourrienne.

"If I had taken it," cried Bonaparte, springing up and seizing his secretary's hand, "I should have found the pasha's money-chests and arms for three hundred thousand men, and I could have aroused and armed all Syria. I would then have marched upon Damascus and Aleppo; I would have augmented my army with all the malcontents; I would have announced the abolishment of servitude, as well as of the tyrannical rule of the pashas; I would have overthrown the Turkish empire, and established in the Orient a vast new empire which would immortalize my name in history, and perhaps I should have returned to Paris by Adrianople and Vienna, after having annihilated the House of Austria."

This, as the reader will perceive, was nothing more nor less than Caesar's plan at the time that he fell beneath the assassin's dagger. It was his war with the Parthians which was to end only in Germany.

There was as great a difference between the man of the 13th Vendémaire and the conqueror of Italy as between the conqueror of Italy and the conqueror of the Pyramids.

Acknowledged in Europe to be the greatest of living generals, he had endeavored to equal, if not surpass, Alexander, Hannibal, and Caesar in the same countries and upon the same shores where they had fought, and he had surpassed them, inasmuch as he had tried to do what they had only dreamed of doing.

"What would have become of Europe," says Pascal, referring to Cromwell's death, "if that grain of sand had not been in his entrails?"

To what heights might not Bonaparte have risen if Saint Jean d'Acre had not stood in his way?

While his thoughts were still busy with the future, his gaze was attracted by a black speck between two mountains in the Carmel chain, and as he gazed the black speck gradually became larger and larger, and soon he perceived that it was one of the dromedary corps which he himself had established to pursue fugitives after a battle. The man was coming as fast as his dromedary would bring him.

Bonaparte drew a glass from his pocket, and after having looked intently for a moment, said:

"Good! we shall hear from Egypt now."

He stood up, and the messenger must have recognized him, for he immediately turned his dromedary toward the hill, and Bonaparte immediately went down, and seating himself upon a stone, waited.

"Whence do you come?" shouted Bonaparte, as soon as he thought the man would be likely to hear him.

"From upper Egypt," was the reply.

"What news?"

"Bad, general."

Bonaparte stamped his foot upon the ground.

"Come here," he cried.

In another minute or two the man had reached Bonaparte. The dromedary knelt, and his rider slid to he ground.

"Here, Citizen General," he said, handing Bonaparte a dispatch.

Bonaparte passed it to Bourrienne.

"Read it," he said.

And Bourrienne read as follows:

"To Commander-in-Chief Bonaparte:

"I do not know that this dispatch will ever reach you, Citizen General, or that you will be in a position to avert the misfortunes that threaten me, even if it does.

"While General Desaix was driving the Mamelukes from the coast of Syout, our flotilla, consisting of the 'Italie' and several other armed vessels laden with artillery and supplies, as well as a large number of sick and wounded, was detained off Beyrout by head winds.

"The flotilla is about to be attacked by Scherif Hassan and three or four thousand men. We are in no condition to resist, but we shall resist.

"We can escape death only by a miracle.

"I am writing this dispatch with the intention of adding the details of the battle as it progresses.

"Hassan began the attack with a sharp fusillade. I have ordered his fire to be returned.

"It is now two o'clock in the afternoon.

"Three o'clock.—After a terrible carnage caused by our artillery, the Arabs are returning for a third time. I have lost nearly half my men.

"Four o'clock.—The Arabs have plunged into the river and secured possession of the small boats.

"I have only twelve men left. All the rest are killed or wounded. I shall wait until the Arabs have crowded upon the 'Italie' and then blow her up with all on board.

"I send this dispatch by a brave and shrewd man, who promises me he will find you wherever you may be, unless he is killed.

"In less than ten minutes all will be over.

"CAPTAIN MORANDI."

"Well?" demanded Bonaparte.

"That is all," said Bourrienne.

"But Morandi?"

"Blew himself up, general, as he said he would," replied the messenger.

"And you?"

"Oh, I didn't wait for that. After I had put the dispatch carefully away in my tobacco-box, I swam under water to a place on the river bank where I could hide myself in the long grass. As soon as it was dark I started for the Moslem camp, creeping cautiously along on all fours. I soon came to a sleeping Arab, and after plunging a dagger into him and taking his dromedary, I started off at a gallop."

"And you have come all the way from Beyrout?"

"Yes, Citizen General."

"Without any accident?"

"If you call shots, fired either by me or at me, accidents, then I've had plenty of them, and my camel likewise. We have been hit four times between us—he three times in the side, and I once in the shoulder. We have been hungry, and we have been thirsty. He has eaten nothing at all, and I—I have lived chiefly on horseflesh; but here we are at last."

"But Morandi?" repeated Bonaparte.

"*Dame*! as he put the match to the powder himself, I imagine it would be hard work to find a piece of him as big as a hazel-nut."

"And the 'Italie?'"

"Oh, there isn't enough left of the 'Italie' to make a box of matches."

"You were right, my friend; this is, indeed, bad news. Bourrienne, you will think me superstitious, but did you notice the name of the vessel that was blown up?"

"Yes; the 'Italie.'"

"Well mark my words, Bourrienne, Italy is lost to France. I am positive of it. My presentiments never deceive me."

Bourrienne shrugged his shoulders.

"What connection do you suppose there can be between a ship that is blown up on the Nile—eight hundred leagues from France—and Italy?" he asked.

"You will see—you will see!" responded Bonaparte.

Then after a moment's silence, he added, pointing to the messenger:

"Take this man with you, Bourrienne; give him thirty *tataris*, and ask him to tell you the story of the battle of Beyrout."

"If you would give me a glass of water instead of the thirty *tataris*, citizen, I should be very grateful."

"You shall have your thirty *tataris* and a whole pitcher of water, and you should have a sword of honor besides if you hadn't Pichegru's already."

"He knows me," exclaimed the messenger, with evident delight.

"Brave fellows like you are not easily forgotten, Falou; but if you want to keep out of the guard house, don't fight any more duels."

CHAPTER XVI

THE RETREAT

In order to conceal its movements from the enemy, as well as to avoid the heat of the day, the army began its retreat at night.

Orders had been given to follow the shore of the Mediterranean, so the troops might have the benefit of the sea air.

Prior to the hour of departure, Bonaparte summoned Bourrienne, and dictated an order to the effect that all who were able should go on foot, leaving the horses, mules, and camels for the sick and wounded.

Some trifling incident oftentimes gives a better idea of the state of a man's mind than the most elaborate description.

Bonaparte had just dictated the above order to Bourrienne, when his groom, Vigogne, the elder, came into the tent, and saluting respectfully, said:

"General, which horse do you reserve for yourself?"

Bonaparte glared at him for an instant, then striking him across the face with his riding-whip, he exclaimed:

"Didn't you hear the order, idiot? Every one is to go on foot, myself as well as all the others. Go!"

And Vigogne required no second bidding.

There were three men sick of the plague at Mount Carmel. They were too ill to be moved; so they were left to the care of the Carmelite brothers and to the generosity of the Turks. Unfortunately, Sidney Smith was not here to save them, so the Turks put them to death. This news reached Bonaparte when the French army had gone only two leagues, and he flew into a fit of rage to which the blow inflicted, upon Vigogne had been only the prelude. He stopped the artillery wagons at once and distributed torches to the army, with orders to light them and set fire to all the small towns, villages, and hamlets.

The barley was fully ripe, and they set fire to that also.

It was a terrible but magnificent sight. The entire coast for leagues was in flames, and the sea reflected the tremendous ocean of fire like a gigantic mirror. The army seemed to be marching between two walls of flame, so faithfully did the sea reproduce the appearance of the coast. The beach being bare sand, was the only thing not on fire, and looked like a bridge thrown over the Cocytus.

But the beach, too, presented a lugubrious aspect. The men who were most severely wounded were carried on litters; the others were mounted on mules, horses, or camels. It so happened that Faraud, who had been wounded the night before, had been given the horse Bonaparte usually rode, and the general recognized both the than and his mount.

"Ah! so that is the way you are doing your twenty-four hours in the guard-house!" he called out to him.

"I'll do them at Cairo," answered Faraud.

"Have you anything there to drink, Goddess of Reason?" inquired Bonaparte.

"Will you have a glass of brandy, Citizen General?"

Bonaparte shook his head.

"Wait," cried the goddess. "I know what you want."

And after fumbling about in the bottom of her little cart, she added:

"Here, take this."

As she spoke, she handed him a water-melon from the gardens of Carmel.

It was a royal gift.

Bonaparte stopped and sent for Kléber, Bon, and Vial to share his good fortune. Lannes, wounded in the head, passed on a mule, and Bonaparte made him stop, and the five generals finished their breakfast by draining a big jug of water and drinking to the health of the Goddess of Reason.

On resuming his place at the head of the column, Bonaparte was really alarmed.

A devouring thirst, the total absence of water, the excessive heat, and the fatiguing march through the burning sand had completely demoralized the men, and soon caused utter indifference and even cruel selfishness to entirely supersede all generous and noble sentiments.

And so it went on day after day.

First they began to rid themselves of those who were sick with the plague, under the pretext that it was dangerous to carry them.

Then the turn of the wounded came.

The unfortunate men pleaded:

"I have not got the plague; I am only wounded!"

It was in vain that they displayed their old wounds or even inflicted new ones upon themselves.

The soldiers would not even turn their heads to look at them.

"Your time has come," they said, and went on.

Bonaparte shuddered with horror as he saw all this.

He called a halt, and compelled all the able-bodied men who were on horses, mules, or dromedaries to relinquish them to the sick.

On the 20th of May they reached Tentoura.

The heat was suffocating, and they hunted in vain for a patch of grass or a tree to shelter them from the blinding glare. They stretched themselves out on the sand; but it burned them like fire. Men were continually falling to rise no more. A wounded man on a litter was begging piteously for water.

Bonaparte approached him.

"Whom have you there?" he inquired of the men who were carrying the litter.

"We don't know," answered one of the men. "He has one double epaulette; that is all we know about him."

The moaning and the begging for water ceased.

"Who are you?" asked Bonaparte.

But the wounded man made no reply.

Bonaparte lifted a corner of the sheet that shaded the litter, and saw Croisier.

"My poor boy!" he exclaimed.

Croisier began to sob bitterly.

"Come, come! have courage," said Bonaparte kindly.

"Ah!" said Croisier, lifting himself up on one elbow, "do you think I am crying because I am going to die? I am weeping because you once called me a coward, and it was because you called me a coward that I tried my best to get killed."

"But I sent you a sword since that," said Bonaparte. "Didn't Roland give it to you?"

"Here it is," cried Croisier, seizing the weapon which was lying beside him, and putting it to his lips. "These men here know I want it to be buried with me. Order them to do it, general."

And the wounded man clasped his hands imploringly.

Bonaparte dropped the corner of the sheet, gave the desired order, and walked sadly away.

Soon after leaving Tentoura the next day they came to an immense quicksand. There was no other road, so the artillery, too, was obliged to traverse it. The guns sunk deep into it; so the soldiers laid the sick and wounded on the edge of the quicksand for a time while they attached all the horses to the gun-carriages and wagons. But it was in vain. The wagons and cannon had sunken too deep in the sand. All the able-bodied soldiers begged to be allowed to make one last attempt to move them, and they did; but, like the horses, they exhausted their strength to no purpose.

They wept as they abandoned the guns they had so often blessed—the guns which had so often witnessed their triumphs, and whose thunder had made all Europe tremble.

On the 22d of May they slept at Caesarea.

So many sick and wounded had died on the journey that horses were more plentiful.

Bonaparte himself, who was far from well, had nearly died of fatigue the day before, and his brother-officers were so persistent in their entreaties that he finally consented to mount a horse. He was only a few hundred yards from Caesarea, when just at daybreak, a man who was hiding in some bushes by the road-side, fired almost point-blank at him, but missed him.

The soldiers, who happened to be near the commander-in-chief, darted into the bushes and dragged out the man, a native of Nabloos, who was condemned to be shot on the spot.

Four men pushed him toward the sea with their carbines, then they pulled the triggers; but not one of the four weapons went off, for the night before had been damp and the powder was wet.

The Syrian, amazed to find himself still alive, speedily recovered his presence of mind, and throwing himself into the sea, swam swiftly to a reef out of rifle range.

In the first moment of stupefaction the soldiers stood and watched him without remembering to fire at him; but Bonaparte, who knew what a bad effect it would have upon these superstitious people if such an attempt went unpunished, ordered a whole platoon to fire at him.

They obeyed; but the man was out of range, and the bullets fell hissing into the sea without reaching the rock upon which the would-be assassin had taken refuge.

The Syrian drew a dagger from his breast and made a threatening movement with the weapon.

Bonaparte ordered the men to put a charge and a half in their guns and fire again.

"It is not worth while," said Roland, "I am going."

As he spoke, he threw off his clothes, retaining only his drawers.

"No, no, Roland," interposed Bonaparte. "I will not have you stake your life against that of an assassin."

But either he did not hear him or did not want to hear him, for Roland had already snatched a dagger from the Sheik of Aher, and placing it between his teeth, had plunged into the sea.

The soldiers, who knew the young captain to be the most daring officer in the army, shouted, "Bravo!" and Bonaparte was obliged to remain an unwilling witness of the duel that was about to take place.

The Syrian, when he saw only one person coming toward him, attempted no further flight, but calmly awaited his approach. Standing there on the rock, with one hand tightly clinched and his dagger in the other, he looked like the statue of Spartacus upon its pedestal.

Roland swam straight toward him.

The Syrian made no attempt to attack him until he had gained a foothold on the rock. He even stepped chivalrously back as far as the size of the rock would permit.

Roland emerged from the water handsome and vigorous, and dripping like a sea-god.

The two men stood facing each other. The rock that was to serve as their gladiatorial arena looked like the shell of an immense turtle protruding out of the water.

The spectators expected a prolonged and scientific combat, in which each antagonist would take good care to give his opponent no advantage.

But they were mistaken.

Roland had no sooner regained his feet and shaken off the water that blinded him as it dripped from his hair than, without seeming to think of protecting himself from his opponent's dagger, he sprung upon him, not as one man springs upon another, but as a tiger springs upon his prey.

The blades of two daggers flashed, in the sunlight; then, as if suddenly hurled from their pedestal, the two men fell into the water with a tremendous splash.

Soon one head appeared above the surface—the fair head of Roland.

Seizing a jagged point of the rock with one hand, he pulled himself up until he could rest his knee upon it, and finally straightened himself up, holding in his left hand, by a thick lock of hair, the head of his antagonist.

He looked very much as Perseus must have looked after he cut off the Gorgon's head.

A deafening shout rose from the spectators, and reached the ears of Roland, around whose lips a proud smile played; then, replacing the dagger between his teeth, he sprung into the sea and swam to the shore.

The army had halted. The soldiers forgot the heat and their thirst in watching the combat; the wounded forgot their wounds, and even the dying found strength to raise themselves upon their elbows.

Roland paused about ten feet from Bonaparte.

"Here is the head of your would-be assassin," he exclaimed, casting the bloody trophy at the general's feet.

Bonaparte recoiled in spite of himself; but Roland walked straight to his clothes, and began putting them on as calmly as if he had just emerged from an ordinary bath.

CHAPTER XVII

IN WHICH WE SEE THAT BONAPARTE'S PRESENTIMENTS DID NOT DECEIVE HIM

The French reached Jaffa on the 24th.

They remained there through the 25th, 26th, 27th, and 28th.

Jaffa was, indeed, a most unlucky city for Napoleon.

The reader will remember the four thousand prisoners captured there who could neither be kept, nor fed, nor sent to Cairo, but who had to be, and were, shot.

But a still graver and more deplorable necessity awaited Bonaparte on his return.

There was a hospital for soldiers stricken with the plague at Jaffa.

We have in the Musée a superb picture of Gros, representing Bonaparte touching the plague-stricken veterans at Jaffa.

The picture is no less beautiful because it depicts an incident that never occurred.

That is what Monsieur Thiers says, and we, who belong to the coterie of mere insignificant romancers, regret to find ourselves differing with that giant among historians on yet another point.

It is the celebrated author of "The Revolution," as well as the "The Consulate and the Empire," who is speaking.

"When we reached Jaffa, Bonaparte blew up the fortifications. There was a hospital for soldiers ill with the plague in the city. To carry these men away was an utter impossibility; to leave them there was to expose them to certain death, either from sickness, hunger, or cruelty of the enemy; so Bonaparte told Doctor Desgenettes that it would be much more humane to give them opium than to permit them to live, whereupon the doctor made that much commended response: 'It is my trade to cure, not kill.' The opium was not administered, and the occurrence gave rise to an outrageous slander, which has since been entirely refuted."

I humbly beg Monsieur Thiers' pardon, but this reply of Desgenettes, whom I knew well, like Larrey and all of the Egyptians—as they were the companions of my father on that famous expedition—is as apocryphal as that of Cambronne.

"Heaven preserve me from slandering any one"—were the words Monsieur Thiers uses—"above all, the man who illumined the first half of the nineteenth century with the blaze of his glory." But when we come to Pichegru and the Duc d'Enghien, the reader will see whether I merely re-echo infamous rumors or not; but truth is one and indivisible, and it is the duty of a person who addresses the public to speak the truth boldly.

We remarked a moment ago that the picture by Gros represents an incident that never occurred, and we will prove it.

Here is Davoust's report, written under the very eyes and at the bidding of the commander-in-chief:

"The army reached Jaffa on the 24th of May, and remained there through the 25th, 26th, and 27th of that month. The fortifications of Jaffa were demolished, and all the artillery in the town was thrown into the sea. The wounded were sent away both by sea and land. There were very few ships; so to give time to complete the evacuation by land, we were obliged to postpone the departure of the army until the 28th.

"Kléber's division formed the rear guard, and did not leave Jaffa until the 29th."

You see there is not a word said about the plague or about any visit to the hospital, nor is there any allusion to it in any of the other official reports.

Yet it would have been ill-timed modesty, most assuredly on the part of Bonaparte, whose eyes had been turned toward France ever since they had been turned away from the East, to make no allusion to a deed which would have done honor, not so much to his reason, perhaps, as to his daring.

Moreover, this is the account that Bourrienne—who was an eye-witness, and a very appreciative eye-witness—gives of the affair:

"Bonaparte visited the hospital. It was filled with wounded men—men whose limbs had been amputated, me who were afflicted with ophthalmia, and who were moaning piteously, and soldiers sick with the plague. The beds of these last were on the right-hand side as we entered the first ward. I was walking beside the general, and I solemnly affirm that I did not see him touch a single one of the plague-stricken patients. Why should he have done so? They were in the last stages of the disease, and not one of them spoke.

"Bonaparte knew perfectly well that he was not exempt from contagion. Could he suppose that Chance, Fortune—call it what you will—would especially interfere in his behalf? It certainly had not aided him sufficiently in his plans for the last two months for him to place much confidence in it now.

"Was it likely, I ask, that he would have thus exposed himself to certain death; he who was so necessary—I may truly say, so indispensable—to his army, he upon whom the lives of all who had survived the recent disaster unquestionably depended; who had just given abundant proof of their unalterable courage by their devotion, their sufferings, and their heroic endurance of privations of every kind; who were still doing all he could possibly ask of them and who trusted only in him?"

That is the voice of logic; but here is something more convincing.

Bonaparte walked swiftly through the rooms, tapping his boot-top with the riding whip he held in his hand.

As he strode along, these words fell from his lips:

"The fortifications are destroyed. Luck was against me at Saint Jean d'Acre. I must hasten back to Egypt to protect it from approaching enemies. The Turks will be here in a few hours. Let all who are strong enough to be moved come with us. They can be carried on litters and horses."

There were not more than sixty sick with the plague. Everything that has been said about any larger number is an exaggeration.

Their complete prostration, their silence and extreme weakness, indicated the near approach of death.

To make any attempt to remove them in that state would have been certain to spread the plague among the rest of the army.

"If one longs for continual conquest, fame, and brilliant achievements, one must accept one's share of ill-fortune as well; and when we think we have found something to censure in the acts of a great military leader who is driven to dire extremities by reverses of fortune, it would be advisable for us, before passing judgment, to inquire into the condition of affairs, and to ask ourselves, with our hands on our hearts, if we might not have done exactly as he did under the same circumstances. In that case we must pity rather than blame the man who is compelled to do something that seems cruel, for victory, to speak frankly, cannot be won except with these of similar horrors."

Here is another writer who has every possible interest in telling the truth.

Listen to what he says:

"He ordered an investigation to be made as to what it would be best to do. Those deputized to perform this duty reported there were only seven or eight plague-stricken patients, all so far advanced with the disease that they could not live more than twenty-four hours, and who would be sure to spread the disease among all with whom they came in contact. Several even begged for speedy death, and Bonaparte really felt that it would be a deed of charity to shorten their sufferings by a few hours."

Do you still doubt? Then Napoleon shall speak for himself, and in the first person:

"What man would not have preferred immediate death to the horror of living exposed to the tortures of those barbarians? If my son—and I believe I love him as devotedly as any man can love his children—were in a situation similar to that of those unfortunate creatures, I should be strongly in favor of doing the same to him, and if I were placed in such a position myself, I should certainly insist that it be done to me."

Nothing could be clearer than those few lines, it seems to me. How did it happen that Monsieur Thiers failed to read them? And if he did read them, why does he deny a fact which is admitted by the person who would certainly be most interested in concealing it?

Thus we establish the fact, not for the sake of blaming Bonaparte—who could not have acted otherwise than he did—but to prove to the advocates of pure history that pure history is not always *true* history.

In returning to Cairo, the little army followed the same route it had taken on leaving it; but the heat became more and more intolerable each day. When they left Gaza, the thermometer indicated a temperature of 35 degrees centigrade, and if the mercury was placed on the sand, it rose to 45 degrees.

In the middle of the desert, just before they reached El-Arich, Bonaparte noticed two soldiers filing up a grave, and he thought he recognized them as the same men with whom he had talked a fortnight before. And in fact when they were questioned, they said that they were the same men he had seen carrying Croisier's litter, and that the poor fellow had lust died from lockjaw.

"Did you bury his sword with him?" asked Bonaparte.

"Yes," they both replied, as if with one voice.

"Are you sure?" insisted Bonaparte.

One of the men stooped down over the grave, and thrusting away the sand with his hand, pulled the hilt of a sword to the surface.

"Very well, finish your work," said the commander-in-chief.

He remained until the grave was filled up; then, fearing it might be violated, he said:

"Will some one volunteer to remain here until the army has passed?"

"I will," responded a voice that seemed to come from the clouds.

Bonaparte turned and saw Falou perched upon his dromedary.

"How does it happen that you are riding a dromedary, when every one else is on foot?" he asked.

"Because two men have died of the plague on my dromedary, and no one will ride on it."

"So you are not afraid of the plague, it seems."

"I am not afraid of anything, Citizen General."

"Very well, I'll remember that. Go and find your friend Faraud. I want both of you to come and see me after we reach Cairo."

"We will be there, Citizen General."

Bonaparte cast a lingering glance at Croisier's grave.

"Rest in peace, poor Croisier!" he murmured. "Your humble grave will not often be disturbed."

CHAPTER XVIII

ABOUKIR

On the 14th of June, 1799, after a retreat across the burning sands of Syria, almost as disastrous as that later retreat from Moscow across the snows of Beresina, Bonaparte entered Cairo in the midst of an immense concourse of people.

The sheik, who was expecting him, presented him with a magnificent horse and the Mameluke Roustan.

In his bulletin to the army, issued from Saint Jean d'Acre, Bonaparte had declared that he was returning to Egypt to prevent the landing of a Turkish army that had been gathered on the Isle of Rhodes.

He had been correctly informed on this point, and on the 11th of July the look-outs at Alexandria signaled that there were seventy-six vessels in the offing, twelve of which were war-ships flying the Ottoman flag.

General Marmont, who was in command at Alexandria, dispatched courier after courier to Cairo and Rosette. He also requested the commander at Ramanieh to forward all the troops at his disposal, and himself sent two hundred men to Aboukir to reenforce that place.

That very same day Colonel Godard, the commander at Aboukir, wrote to Marmont:

"The Turkish fleet is anchored in the harbor. My men and I will fight until the very last man falls, rather than yield."

The 12th and 13th of July were employed by the enemy in hastening the arrival of several belated battalions.

On the evening of the 13th there were one hundred and thirty vessels in the roadstead, of which thirteen were ships of seventy-four guns each, nine frigates, and seventeen gunboats. All the others were transports.

On the evening of the following day Godard's promise had been fulfilled. He and his men were dead and the redoubt taken.

Thirty-five men remained shut up in the fort, under command of Colonel Vinache, and they held the fort for two days against the entire Turkish army.

Bonaparte heard all this while he was still at the Pyramids.

He immediately started for Ramanieh, reaching that place on the 19th of July.

The Turks, now masters both of the redoubt and of the fort, had landed all their artillery. Marmont, who was in Alexandria with only eighteen hundred troops of the line and two hundred marines with which to resist the Turks, sent courier after courier to Bonaparte.

Fortunately, instead of marching upon Alexandria, as Marmont feared, or upon Rosette, as Bonaparte had apprehended, the Turks, with their usual indolence, contented themselves with occupying the peninsula and throwing up a long line of intrenchments to the left of the redoubt and bordering on Lake Madieh.

Five or six thousand feet in front of the redoubt they fortified two mamelons, stationing a thousand men in one of them and two thousand in the other.

They had eighteen thousand men all told; but these eighteen thousand men seemed to have come to Egypt for the express purpose of being besieged.

Bonaparte waited for Mustapha, but finding that he showed no disposition to advance, he, Bonaparte, resolved to take the initiative; so on the 23d he ordered the French troops, which were now only two hours' march from the Turkish army, to advance.

Murat's cavalry and three of General Destaing's battalions, with two pieces of artillery, composed the center.

General Rampon's division was on the left. This commander had Generals Fugière and Lanusse under him.

The division of General Lannes advanced along the shore of Lake Madieh on the right.

Stationed between Alexandria and the army, with two squadrons of cavalry and one hundred dromedaries, Davoust had been ordered to hold in check Mourad Bey or any other general who might attempt to come to the assistance of the Turks, and also to keep communication open between Alexandria and the army.

Kléber, who was also expected, was to assume command of the reserves.

The French army came in sight of the intrenchments before the Turks even suspected their close proximity.

General Destaing, who commanded them, marched straight toward the fortified hillock on the right, while Murat's cavalry abandoned their position between the two hills and rode around the right hill to cut off the retreat of the Turks attacked by General Destaing.

Meanwhile, Lannes, had started toward the hill on the left, which was defended by two thousand Turks, and Murat sent two hundred more of his cavalry around to the other side of this hill.

Destaing and Lannes attacked almost simultaneously and with equal success. The two positions were carried at the point of the bayonet, and the fleeing Turks meeting the French cavalry, threw themselves into the sea to escape capture.

Destaing, Lannes, and Murat then proceeded toward the village which formed the center of the peninsula.

Just then a column left the Turkish camp at Aboukir, with the evident intention of coming to the assistance of the village.

Murat drew his saber—which he seldom or never did

until the very last minute—and charging upon the column, drove it back to Aboukir.

Meanwhile, Lannes and Destaing had captured the village, from which Turks fled in every direction, only to meet Murat's cavalry returning.

Four or five hundred corpses already strewed the battle-field. The French had but one man wounded. He was a mulatto, a compatriot of my father, a commander in the Hercules Guides.

Bonaparte could have shut the Turks up in Aboukir and harassed them with shells and bombs while waiting for Kléber's and Regnier's divisions to come up, but he preferred to deal a decisive blow; so he ordered the army to march straight upon the second line of defenses.

It was still Lannes and Destaing, supported by Lanusse, who did most of the fighting, and who are entitled to the honors of the day.

The redoubt at Aboukir had been built by the English, and was consequently constructed on the most approved scientific principles.

It was defended by nine or ten thousand Turks, and was connected with the sea by a causeway.

They had not had time enough to dig far in the other direction, however, so it was not connected with the neighboring lake.

Bonaparte ordered an attack to be made on the front and right. Murat, who was in ambush in a grove of palm-trees, was to make an attack on the left, and cross the space where there was no causeway, though this open space was not only occupied by the enemy, but likewise swept by a heavy artillery fire.

The battle, consequently, was sure to be desperate one, for the Turks realized that they were hemmed in by the sea in front and a wall of French bayonets behind.

A heavy cannonade opened upon the redoubt and the line of intrenchments on the right was the signal for a general attack. Bonaparte ordered General Fugière to advance in order to turn the enemy's right if possible, while the Thirty-second was to hold the enemy in check and support the Eighteenth.

Noting these arrangements, the Moslems left their intrenchments and advanced to meet us.

On perceiving this fact, the French troops uttered an exultant shout—for this was exactly what they wanted—and rushed upon the enemy with bayonets lowered.

The Turks discharged their guns first, then the brace of pistols each of them carried, and finally drew their sabers; but our soldiers, undaunted, charged upon them with the bayonets.

Not until then did the Turks realize what manner of men and weapons they had to deal with, and with their guns slung across their shoulders, and their sabers hanging by their cords, they began a hand-to-hand fight, trying to tear from the enemy's rifles those terrible bayonets which pierced their breasts just as they were stretching out their hands to seize them.

But nothing could stop the gallant Eighteenth.

It continued to advance at the same pace, driving the Turks back to the foot of the intrenchments, after which it attempted to carry them by storm, but were finally driven back by a terrific fire.

General Fugière, who conducted the attack, was wounded slightly in the head by a bullet, but he continued to urge on his men; but when a ball carried away his arm he was obliged to pause.

Adjutant General Lalong, who came up just then with a battalion, made an heroic attempt to induce the men to brave this hurricane of fire. Twice he led them into it, and twice they were repulsed. The third time he sprung forward, and was about to leap into the intrenchments, when he fell, shot dead.

For a long time, Roland, who was standing near Bonaparte, had been begging for a command of some kind. At last the general-in-chief, feeling that the moment for making a supreme effort had come, turned to his aid, and said:

"Very well, then go!"

"Thirty-second Brigade!" shouted Roland; and the brave survivors of Saint Jean d'Acre, headed by their major, rushed toward the speaker.

In the foremost rank was Sub-lieutenant Faraud, whose wound was now healed.

Meanwhile another attempt to dislodge the enemy had been made by Brigadier General Morange; but he, too, had been driven back wounded, leaving thirty men on the glacis and in the trenches.

The Turks felt sure that the victory was theirs, and forgetting everything else in their eagerness to cut off heads—for which they received fifty paras apiece—they left the redoubt to begin that bloody work.

Roland called the attention of his indignant soldiers to the fact.

"All our men are not even dead," he cried. "There are many wounded among them. Let us save them or die!"

Almost at the same instant Murat saw through the smoke what was going on, and dashing forward under the heavy fire of the artillery, cut the redoubt off from the village by his cavalry, and then rushed upon the men who were engaged in their ghastly work of cutting off heads, while Roland attacked them in front, dashing upon the Turks with his accustomed recklessness, and mowing down the bloody harvesters at a fearful rate.

Bonaparte perceived that the Turks were placed at a great disadvantage by this two-fold attack, and sent Lannes also forward with two battalions to attack the Moslems on the left flank.

Hard pressed on all sides, the Turks tried to reach the village; but Murat and his cavalry were between that and the redoubt, and Roland and the Thirty-second Brigade being behind them and Lannes on one side of them, their only refuge was the sea, and into this they plunged, frantic with terror; for as they were not in the habit of showing any mercy to their prisoners, they preferred the sea, which gave them a chance of reaching their ships, to death at the hands of the despised Christians.

The French were masters of the two hillocks, where they began the attack of the hamlet where the remnant of the troops that had defended the knolls had taken refuge and of the redoubt which had cost so many brave men their lives. They had now reached the camp and the Turkish reserves, and both soon succumbed to their opponents.

Nothing could stop our men now, for they were intoxicated by the carnage they had already committed.

Murat and his cavalry swooped down on the pasha's guard like a whirlwind, a hurricane, a simoon.

Ignorant of the result of the battle, Mustapha, on hearing the shouts and confusion, placed himself at the head of his *icoglans* and rushed upon the French. Encountering Murat, he fired upon him at close range, inflicting a slight wound; but Murat, with the first blow of his saber, cut off two of his fingers, and would have cut off his head with the second, if an Arab had not thrown himself in front of the pasha and received the blow. Mustapha then surrendered his cimeter, and Murat sent him a prisoner to Bonaparte.

See Gros's superb painting.

A small remnant of the army took refuge in the fort; all the rest were killed or drowned.

Never since two armies first confronted each other has such utter annihilation of one contending force been witnessed. The two hundred janissaries and one hundred men shut up in the fort were all that remained of the eighteen thousand Turks who had landed.

Kléber came up just at the close of the battle.

He asked the result of the day's fighting, and then inquired where Bonaparte was.

Bonaparte was standing on the furthermost point of the peninsula, gazing at the gulf which had swallowed up the French fleet—that is to say, his only hope of returning to France.

Kléber approached him, and taking him by the arm, exclaimed:

"General, you are as great as the world!"

CHAPTER XIX

DEPARTURE

During the year that this eighth crusade lasted, the ninth —if we count the double attempt of Saint Louis as two— Napoleon had done all that it was possible for any human being to do.

He had taken Alexandria, had vanquished the Mamelukes at Chebreiss and the Pyramids, taken Cairo, conquered the Delta, completed the subjugation of upper Egypt, taken Gaza and Jaffa, destroyed the army of Djezzar at Mount Tabor, and finally annihilated a second Turkish army at Aboukir.

The tri-color had floated triumphantly over the Nile and the Jordan; but he was ignorant of what was going on in France, and that is why he was gazing abstractedly at the sea which had swallowed up his ships.

Soon he sent for Falou, and questioned him again in regard to the fight at Beyrout, the disaster which had befallen the flotilla, and the loss of the "Italie," and as he did so, his presentiments became more disquieting than ever.

At last he called Roland.

"I feel strongly tempted to open a new career for you, my dear Roland," he remarked.

"What is it, may I ask?"

"That of a diplomat."

"An appalling idea, truly, general."

"And yet you must consent to try it."

"What! you will not permit me to decline?"

"No."

"Say on, then."

"I am going to send you to Sidney Smith with a flag of truce."

"And my instructions?"

"Are to ascertain what is going on in France, and you must do your best to distinguish that which is true from that which is false in what the commodore tells you. Not an easy matter, by any means, I assure you."

"I will do my best; but what is to be the ostensible object of my mission?"

"To arrange for an exchange of prisoners. The English have twenty-five of our men; we have two hundred and fifty Turks, and we will give them the two hundred and fifty Turks if they will agree to give us back our twenty-five Frenchmen."

"When am I to go?"

"To-day."

It was the 26th of July.

Roland went and returned with a complete file of newspapers, for Sidney had recognized him as the hero of Saint Jean d'Acre, and had willingly consented to give him full particulars of what was going on in Europe. Then, perceiving Roland's incredulity, he had given him all the French, English, and German newspapers he had with him on the "Tiger."

The news these papers contained was truly appalling.

The Republic, defeated at Sockah and Magnano, had lost Germany at Sockah and Italy at Magnano.

Massena had secured an impregnable position on the Albis. The Apennines had been invaded, and the Var threatened.

The next day, on seeing Roland again, Bonaparte exclaimed:

"Well?"

"Well?" repeated the young man.

"I knew very well that Italy was lost to us."

"We will have to take it again, that is all."

"We will try," responded Bonaparte. "Call Bourrienne."

Bourrienne was summoned.

"Ask Berthier where Gantheaume is," said Bonaparte.

"He is at Ramanieh, superintending the preparation of the fleet that is to start for upper Egypt."

"Are you sure?"

"I received a letter from him yesterday."

"I need a brave and trusty messenger," said Bonaparte, turning to Roland. "Find Falou and his dromedary."

Roland departed on his errand.

"Write this, Bourrienne," continued Bonaparte:

"'As soon as Admiral Gantheaume receives this, he will report to General Bonaparte.

"'*July 26th* 1799   BOURRIENNE.'"

Ten minutes afterward Roland returned with Falou and his dromedary. Bonaparte surveyed his messenger with evident satisfaction.

"Is your animal in as good condition as you are?" he asked.

"My dromedary and I are in a condition to make our twenty-five leagues a day, general."

"I only ask you to make twenty."

"A mere trifle."

"You are to take this letter to Ramanieh."

"It will reach its destination this evening."

"Read the address."

"To Admiral Gantheaume."

"And now if you should lose it——"

"I shall not lose it."

"We must provide for any contingency. Listen to its contents."

"It is not very long, I hope?"

"It contains but one sentence."

"Very well, then, let me hear the sentence."

"'As soon as Admiral Gantheaume receives this, he will report to General Bonaparte.'"

"That is easy enough to remember."

"Go then!"

Falou made his dromedary kneel, climbed upon his hump, and started the animal off at a brisk trot.

"I'm off!" he shouted.

And in fact he was already some distance away.

The next evening he returned.

"The admiral is following me," he said.

The admiral arrived during the night. Bonaparte had not gone to bed. Gantheaume found him busily engaged in writing.

"You will fit out two frigates, the 'Murion' and the 'Carrière,' and two smaller vessels, the 'Ravanche' and the 'Fortune,' with provisions to last forty or fifty men two months. Do not say a word about this to any one. You are to accompany me."

Gantheaume withdrew, promising not to lose a moment.

Bonaparte then sent for Murat.

"Italy is lost," he said. "The scoundrels have wasted the fruits of our victories. We must leave here at once. Select five hundred trusty men for me."

Then, turning to Roland, he added:

"And see that Falou and Faraud are included in the number."

Roland bowed his assent.

General Kléber, to whom Bonaparte intended to intrust the command of the army, was requested to come to Rosette to confer with the commander-in-chief on matters of the utmost importance.

Bonaparte made this appointment without the slightest intention of keeping it, however, for he had no desire to hear Kléber's reproaches or to encounter his unpleasant freedom of speech; so he wrote to him all he would have said to him, and pleaded, as an excuse for not keeping his appointment, his fear that the English cruiser might appear at any moment.

The vessel destined for Bonaparte was once more to carry a Caesar and his fortunes; but it was no longer a Caesar sailing eastward to add Egypt to the conquest of Rome, but a Caesar revolving in his mind the mighty projects that led the conqueror of the Gauls to cross the Rubicon.

He was returning to France without recoiling from the thought of overthrowing the government for which he had fought on the 13th of Vendémiaire, and which he had so energetically sustained on the 18th Fructidor.

A scheme of gigantic proportions had faded into nothingness in front of the walls of Saint Jean d'Acre; but an even more ambitious project was absorbing his thoughts as he left Alexandria.

On the 23d of August, a dark and gloomy night, a boat left the Egyptian shore and put Bonaparte aboard the "Murion."

THE END

www.ingramcontent.com/pod-product-compliance
Lightning Source LLC
Chambersburg PA
CBHW060517030426
42337CB00015B/1921